HOZONI
Beautiful Peaceful Valley

by

Joyce White

Horn Publications
P.O. Box 11
Tyrone, NM 88065

2-6-13

For
Earl and Margrey

Earl and Margrey Williams, 1940

Other Nonfiction by Joyce White:

Burro Creek Canyon
Mountain Echoes

Coming Soon

Sand in Our Sandals

Acknowledgments

The late Dick Spencer III, publisher of *The Western Horseman* magazine who accepted my first story.

Craig Degener, editor at *Silver City Sun-News* where my column *Ranch Echoes* appeared.

Roxana Marsh for advice and manuscript preparation.

Deborah Kelly, reader.

Betty J. Verbica, reader and generous supporter.

Jack Sprunk Howell, retired educator (and grandson of a pioneer family).

Holly Wilcox, reader, grateful neighbor and friend.

Maryann S. Berman, advisor.

NikkiO Design, editing and page makeup.

Cookie Stolpe, research librarian at *Miller Library* in Western New Mexico University.

Cokey Millar, for publicity and enthusiastic support.

Mike White, cowboy poet, for permission to use his poem, *The Outhouse.*

Derrall D. Horn, literary agent and publisher, who encouraged me to write this book and promoted it tirelessly.

Contents

CHAPTER ONE

Arizona Homecoming

I woke with a start thinking, Where am I? Then I remembered we were at a motel in Prescott, Arizona and today we were moving to our new cattle ranch! I hopped out of bed and began getting ready.

A few minutes later my husband came back to our room all smiles. Bob was a morning person so I wasn't a bit surprised when he said, "Let's go down to the Dinner Bell Café for breakfast." He would probably order ham and eggs as he often had in years past. "I've fed and exercised Sam", he said. Tending to his animals always came first for Bob.

We drove past the stately old court house with its lush green lawns, then by the 1890s St. Michael Hotel before parking in front of the café. I got out and breathed in the crisp fall air. It was good to be home!

After sliding into a booth we gave our orders to the new waitress. I decided it would be ham and eggs for me, too. This would be a busy day for us. We'd need all the energy we could muster. Our 1,200-mile trip from Missouri had taken its toll and so had all the packing for this move, some of which was in the camper along with Sam, Bob's faithful old cowdog, dating back to our Burro Creek ranching days in NW Arizona.

We were returning to Arizona after six years of ranching in the Ozark Mountains. It had been a good move for us in many ways, but Bob could no longer endure the humidity there and so here we were just two days before the fall roundup and the important cattle count on our newly purchased Hozoni Ranch. The rest of our family would begin to arrive when the ranch escrow closed. First would be my parents, Earl and Marge Williams, then my son Mike and his wife and baby.

We stopped at Safeway to purchase a month's supply of groceries for roundup, then drove toward Skull Valley, a small town consisting of a gas station and county store with a post office in the back of the building. It was a quiet community and the ideal setting for an artist to work. The late George Phippen had his home studio there, and his widow allowed visitors to view some of his work, including the last unfinished work on an easel where he had left it.

We continued on our way to Kirkland, then Kirkland Junction, before turning onto the dirt road which would take us to the ranch, 26 miles farther, passing numerous well-kept outfits with green pastures. When we arrived at the sleeping town of Wagoner, we saw a row of mailboxes that served the area and Bob located a large box belonging to the Hozoni Ranch. We had traveled two and one half hours by this time. We were getting close, Bob informed me. Only eight more miles to go. He stopped the truck to exercise and water Sam, then we proceeded on, crossing the Hassayampa River with cottonwood trees along the banks, now in fall colors mingled with remaining green leaves.

At last, Bob said, "There it is, Gal!" pointing to Hozoni Ranch Headquarters with its cluster of buildings nestled in a narrow brush-covered valley dotted with small green pastures along the way.

I remember my relief at seeing the ranch at last. Pictures of the buildings were all I'd had to study, endlessly, during the six months prior to our move from Missouri, all the while bombarding Bob with questions about this ranch with the Navajo Indian name that he had toured on his search for a new place for our family.

Our heavily loaded four-wheel drive truck crept off the steep mountain road, creaking and groaning, then splashed through a small tree-lined stream before pulling up beside the main ranch house, a large stuccoed building with a screened-in porch. In front of us stood the two- story stage stop which appeared to be in good repair. The boards on the second story had been painted white. I was curious to have a look inside this historic building! Had it once been a relay station on the way to Wickenburg as Bob had been told?

To our right two identical block houses, with a patio between, were enclosed with a chain-link fence. An old English sheepdog came to the front gate, barking to announce our arrival while peeking through thick silver-gray bangs, his blue eyes barely visible. At that moment Sam exchanged barks with the sheep dog. Sam had been a quiet traveler and had remained still outside the café, but this stranger's bark required a response.

A tall, slim woman came out of one of the houses and called, "Come here, Duke." He trotted to her and received a loving pat and a large bone, then he meandered toward his dog house and settled down with a contented sigh to enjoy his treat.

That must be Joe's wife, Lorraine, co-owner of the ranch, I thought.

Our realtor emerged from the second house, broom in hand. Ralph called to us, "Glad you made it okay. The house is almost ready for you. We're hooking up the utilities now." He walked next door to speak to someone before coming to our truck. "Lorraine is fixing you a bite to eat. The men are working cattle today," he said.

I was pleased to hear about lunch. Through the years I'd fed ranch buyers and realtors, as Ralph well knew. Now that courtesy was being returned. At Ralph's request? I wondered. Sorting through our groceries for lunch foods hadn't been exactly appealing—a cup of coffee was. Lorraine and I would be neighbors for several weeks. This was a good start. Counting cattle in such rough country would be difficult and time consuming, and since livestock were included in the ranch price it was vital to tally each cow and calf or make a price adjustment if the number was short.

I remained in the truck while Bob conversed with Ralph. I heard him say to Bob, "I've found a cowboy for you."

"Good!" my husband said. "Sure hope he's worked rough country before. This roundup might be a bit wooly."

"Jay's cowboyed for years. A good hand. He's lonesome for ranch life—been workin' in town lately. He'll be here tomorrow." Ralph returned to the little house.

I sat listening to the chugging light plant and looking at the well-groomed lawn and pink blooming rose bushes; enjoying the moment. A light breeze coming down the valley stirred the cottonwood trees, giving a break in the day that had suddenly turned hot.

Zip! A brilliant orange and black bird flew to a cone-shaped nest in a tree shading the old stage stop. Probably an oriole, I thought. I'll look it up in my bird book, like I've done on our other ranches. First in Burro Creek Canyon, then in the Ozark Mountains in Missouri. Both places had rewarded me with beautiful birds to study and enjoy.

My recall was interrupted when Ralph and George, the ranch foreman, came out to help us unload. I stepped out of our truck and Bob put Sam in the front seat to ensure his safety. The unloading began. First, the large supply of groceries was lugged to the kitchen. Milk, bacon and eggs, chicken, hamburger and roast beef went in the small refrigerator, which I was grateful to have in this sparsely furnished house. The four-burner gas stove, though old, appeared to be in working condition. I'd find out how well the oven worked in the morning, good I hoped, because Bob wanted hot bread with every meal. Hot cakes, biscuits or cornbread. Fortunately, I enjoyed cooking old-time recipes and trying new concoctions as well. "Where do you want this little desk to go?" George asked.

"There on that wall with the bookcase beside it," I pointed to a place in the small living room. That drop leaf desk had been used by Mike when he was homeschooling those eight years in Burro Creek, now it would serve as my writing desk where I hoped to produce saleable short stories now that I was having modest success with selling. The men carried in the bed mattress and put it on the cement floor in the master bedroom. There had been no room for the bed frame in the truck. Suitcases would substitute for dressers; bed sheets for curtains. I located a sheet and draped it over the east window, then set out fresh towels and washcloths in the bathroom.

"You folks packed more in that camper than I ever saw!" George commented. "You should have seen our truck and trailer when we moved to Missouri," I said, laughing.

"I used to move on just one packmule," Bob said wistfully. It was true, he had moved all the way from Texas to Arizona in the 1930s with his string of saddlehorses and a packmule.

When the men had finished unloading the truck, George went up to the corrals where several saddlehorses were receiving new shoes at the old blacksmith shop. "Clang. . .clang" echoed as a horseshoe was being fashioned on the anvil to fit a hoof. Bob and Ralph visited while I unpacked groceries and arranged them on cupboard shelves.

Before sundown, I managed to squeeze out time to inspect the stage station. Built of rocks and wide boards, the two-story building commanded my attention. I swung open the front door on the ground floor to inspect the dark interior. It was cool and pleasant there. Part of that first floor had been dug into the side of a hill, then the walls had been rocked up. How thick they were!

5

About 36 inches, it appeared. Probably this had been a storeroom. Several crude shelves lined the walls. On the overhead beams someone had nailed three wooden hooks which had been fashioned out of sturdy forked limbs. To hang meat from? Already the questions about this historic building were beginning.

To reach the second floor, which was constructed of board and batten, I walked around to the back of the station and noted with pleasure that the weathered door had no knob; rather, a hole and wire bail served as a latch string.

Inside, most of the original floor planking, though worn, was still in good condition in the center. However, along the sides of the room the floor had deteriorated and would need replacing with sturdy wide boards, if they could be found to match. Two rusty wire lines were strung along one wall of the room, and probably had been used for drying jerky in more recent years.

The steps had long since rotted away. I hopped down to the ground and looked at the rough terrain in back of the station, wondering where the horse and mule corral had been located. Was this a meal station or a relay station? What route was this on. . .when was it used? Hozoni, what does it mean? Before long I would begin searching for answers, authentic answers. And because research is rather like a treasure hunt, I would probably find all kinds of interesting surprises along the way.

I returned to the little house to unpack my pots and pans, all the while thinking about the historic stage station and how I could find answers to all my questions.

CHAPTER TWO

Home Sweet Home

I rubbed my back to ease sore muscles as I crawled out of bed. This sleeping arrangement wasn't very satisfactory! It will only be for a short while, I consoled myself. Sleeping on the ground in the old camp in Burro Creek had been more comfortable. Sand was more 'giving' than this cement floor—or maybe it was because I was younger then.

I creaked toward the kitchen to begin breakfast just as Bob came in the back door. He'd been up to the barn already.

"Morning!" I greeted him, more cheerfully than I felt. "What's on for today?" I asked as I mixed a batch of buttermilk biscuit.

"We're going to gather cattle this morning. A short drive. I'll be in early, and George is going to show me how to service the light plant later," he said.

I was pleased to discover how well the oven had baked when I pulled out the pan of golden-brown biscuits. We were eating breakfast at the dinette table when Bob informed me, "George said you can see the main house this afternoon. He and his wife and four kids live over there."

"Good! That will be a nice birthday gift—nicer than that one in Burro Creek seventeen years ago!" I laughed, recalling the first day on roundup when my horse had dumped me.

After breakfast Bob returned to the barn, and I unpacked more cooking utensils and cookbooks, where I found one of Sam's hairs! How it had gotten there I didn't know, but it really didn't matter as I planned to wash everything anyway. My cooking gear had been packed for the move in a large cardboard saddle box now sitting on the living room floor only feet away from the kitchen area, through an arched doorway which gave the house a charming southwestern feeling.

Shortly, I saw four cowboys ride past the house. Joe, the ranch owner, was in the lead, as was customary. Next was George on a gray horse that was wanting to buck. Bob was mounted on a chunky brown horse with white streaks on each side of his tail, aptly named "Skunk" I later learned. Old Sam, our Catahoula leopard cowdog, was following Bob. Sam was a seasoned hand who had helped on many cow drives as a pup in Burro Creek and later in the Ozarks. After the men were gone I decided to walk a short way up the road to get a breath of fresh air and look for wildflowers. It was such a lovely morning! I was delighted to find Indian Paintbrush on the hillside. Its red blooms are among my favorite southwest flowers.

A large roadrunner darted before me and ran up the road on long spindly legs. Those cocky birds like to play games. And according to The World Book Encyclopedia, they are sometimes called "snake birds" because they kill rattlesnakes—I was all for that! But they also kill baby quail. Disagreeable fellows.

A short distance away I found a horned toad, actually a lizard, according to the encyclopedia. I scooped him up to have a close inspection, which he didn't object to at all, though occasionally horned toads will spurt blood from their eyes when disturbed. This little fellow was about three inches long with a light brown body which blended into the terrain nicely. He had the usual horn-like projections on his head and along the ridges of his back. I turned him over and gently stroked under his chin; he closed his eyes and took a little nap. Those delightful creatures make good pets, but I had no desire to confine him so I set him down and he scurried away, quickly blending into the tans and browns on the hillside.

Farther on I came upon a miner's dump where I found several old bottles and some rusty sardine tins, which appeared to have been opened with a pocket knife by the looks of their ragged edge.

When I returned to the house it was still early and I set about baking a peach cobbler for Bob, his favorite dessert. I had packed several quart jars of my home canned peaches for this treat.

"Wanta go up to the corral and see the cattle?" Bob asked.

"Yes!" I replied. I was eager to go with him. Mike and I had always been a part of his cowboy crew in the canyon and he had often shared his plans for herd improvements with us.

At the corral I was pleased to see the Hereford cows were in good shape and so were their calves, though far smaller than the crossbred calves I was used to. But our Charolais bulls that we planned to haul from Missouri would soon change the picture, and give us larger calves, sometimes 50 pounds heavier.

It was mid-afternoon when I walked over to the big house. Entering the large screened porch, I knocked on the front door and was greeted by a smiling young woman. "Come in, Mrs. White," she invited. "I'm Joanie."

I liked her immediately and said, "Please call me Joyce. Thank you for letting me see your home—I've been dying to!"

"I thought you might be," she replied with an understanding smile.

Stepping inside the long living room, I noticed a propane heater in a far corner, on the opposite wall a Franklin stove was sitting on a raised red brick hearth. This large house might need both sources of heat during the winter.

Next, Joanie escorted me to the kitchen and dining room, which was large enough to entertain eight or ten people comfortably. The kitchen had abundant counter space. An old-fashioned flour bin was located near the stove. It would be fun cooking in this kitchen and serving food buffet-style on the long food bar separating the two rooms.

"This back porch is where I have my second refrigerator and washing machine—you're welcome to use it anytime," she generously offered.

Next, we toured the three bedrooms and bath at the end of the house. One of the bedrooms was quite small with an outside entrance and a large window looking east toward the red barns and white board corrals, revealing a magnificent view of Silver Mountain and Castle Rock with its pink boulders jutting skyward. This room had a large closet with several deep shelves. Just right for storing my manuscripts. This can be my studio, I thought as I visualized Navajo rugs and antique furniture in there, a sunny pleasant room where I could write undisturbed or step outside for a breath of fresh air.

"Come over for coffee tomorrow," Joanie invited as I left.

Again I heard the "clang, clang" of horseshoes being shaped on the anvil at the blacksmith shop, and the "chug, chug" of the light plant generating electricity for all the buildings on the ranch, and pumping water into a large storage tank on the hill east of the house, by merely throwing a light switch. Our everyday convenience depended upon that plant. We were soon to discover how costly and time consuming it was to maintain, though.

By sundown we began to wonder if our cowboy was going to come after all, but a short time later we heard the welcome sound of a truck coming off the hill and it soon drove up in back of the house. Bob walked outside to greet Jay, asking, "Have you eaten?" I heard him say he'd had coffee at Kirkland Junction, (not food). I went to my refrigerator and got out groceries to prepare supper for him.

Both men came inside where I was seated at the table in one of the four hard dinette chairs, the only ones in the entire house. Jay removed his old work hat. "Evening, ma'am," he nodded toward me. He was a tall, slim cowboy with brown hair and a ready smile.

My journal reminds me I cooked bacon and eggs and fresh fried potatoes in a cast-iron skillet, after which he thanked me and said, "Just point me toward the bunk house and I'll go bed down." Bob gave him directions and I said, "Breakfast at five o'clock come morning." "Good night then," he replied and strode toward his truck. It roared up the draw and stopped at the bunkhouse.

One by one the lights went out on the ranch. We crawled into our hard bed and I fell asleep mentally arranging our Missouri furniture in the comfortable old ranch house. It was going to be fun settling our things in, when the moving van arrived.

September 20th had been an exciting birthday for me on our new ranch in Peaceful Valley. Now if only the cattle count would go smoothly.

Fresh Peach Cobbler

In a heavy sauce pan, slice 10 or 12 large ripe peaches, peeled. Add:

   4 cups cold water
   1/3 cup sugar dash of salt

Cook until peaches are slightly soft, then pour into Pyrex baking dish. Add:

   1 cup sugar
   3 tablespoons flour
   1 teaspoon cinnamon
   1 teaspoon lemon extract
   lump of butter the size of an egg

Top cobbler with pie crust, putting some scraps in the broth. Sprinkle top with 1 teaspoon sugar. Bake about 1 hour in 350-degree oven. Good hot or cold. Heavenly with homemade ice cream!

CHAPTER THREE

Counting Them Out

The next morning about four o'clock I boiled my usual pot of cowboy coffee and drank a cup to help me wake up. Bob joined me there in the kitchen.

I'd just fried ham and eggs in my cast-iron skillet and was taking a pan of biscuits out of the oven when I heard Jay's knock on the back door.

"Come in!" Bob called.

"Morning," Jay greeted us as he removed his dusty, worn hat, a favorite I surmised. I'd seen many hats like it through the years. They'd been almost a declaration of pride, proof of dusty corral work and long sweaty cow drives. I poured him a cup of java and began dishing up the food, setting a jar of my homemade blackberry jelly from Missouri on the table within easy reach.

"It's good to be back on a ranch," Jay commented. "Nothing can beat this way of life." Soon he would entertain us with stories of wild animals he had tamed: the pet coon who would sit on his shoulder and sneak a cigarette out of his pocket, all the while smiling at him mischievously. And the orphaned fawn he and his wife had raised by feeding it on a baby bottle; also the young javelina that thought Jay's wife was his mother and followed her everywhere.

After breakfast I mixed a batch of yeast bread, kneaded it briskly and set it in a warm spot to rise. Then I decided to walk up to the corral and explore the buildings, taking the footpath across a narrow wooden bridge over the little stream that flowed past the houses. The buildings—some old, some new—were all painted dark red. An old saddle house, with a bench by the door, could be entered from inside the corral. A handy arrangement. I swung open the weathered door and found the room empty, discarded. I wondered why it had been abandoned for the new saddle house located several yards outside the corral. A large two-story hay barn had two horse stalls on the ground floor that could be entered from the corral. An area for storing hay and grain was directly behind the stalls.

As I went out the corral gate I noticed a sign painted on the top board that said: No Smoking. A wise precaution since a carelessly discarded cigarette butt could cause a smoldering fire in dry manure.

A large equipment shed and the new saddle house were located next to the barn; then an old blacksmith shop with a hitching post to restrain a horse while shoeing. An anvil was located there ready to shape horseshoes to fit hooves.

When I went inside the blacksmith shop, I found a colorful Navaho saddle blanket, several cowbells and two cups stored in a gunny sack, ready for a cowboy's coffee break out on the range. I'd seen such items stashed away before, in caves or in tree crotches, where a coffee can served as the pot and enabled a cowboy's repast after a long hard ride.

The cowbells were often used to bell a saddle horse, making him easier to locate while out on the range. One bell still had a leather strap buckled to it. All the buildings were arranged in a large horseshoe pattern.

Leaving the barn area I walked through a small peach orchard, past the chicken house and a dog pen, then up to the garage beside the main ranch house. When I reached our temporary home I could smell the pleasant yeasty aroma of rising bread. It was puffed up nicely and ready to be fashioned into buns. They would be tasty with the pinto beans I'd soaked overnight. I drained them, added fresh water, ham bits and diced onion, then a dash of garlic salt and chili powder before putting them on to boil.

I remember I was kneading the bread dough when the story "A Horse of His Own" began to jell in my mind. Hurriedly, I finished lunch preparations and went to the little desk to begin writing. An hour and a half later a first draft was written, leaving me happy and excited over the recall of Mike's first horse and his thrill over receiving him.

It wasn't long after that when Bob and Jay arrived home for lunch and they had surprising news: Everyone on the ranch was to take the day off from gathering cattle the next day. Jay would be going home to see his family, and Bob and I could drive down to Bagdad to visit longtime friends, Betty and Gene Criner. In Burro Creek, we had always worked the entire lower country without a break, but I reminded myself that this was a larger outfit and every rancher has his own way of working. Anyway, we were delighted to have this time off! And I could buy fresh meat at the company store. The ranch hadn't butchered a beef for roundup, although it was an old-time custom we had hoped would apply on the Hozoni.

Lack of meat to prepare for roundup meals was unhandy and we were disappointed, of course, but as soon as roundup was over and we'd taken ownership we would butcher, hanging the meat several days outside at night to age and in the cool stage house during the day wrapped in a tarp. This method of aging tenderized the meat and improved flavor. Nothing equals this meat. We planned to make some jerky, also, to tuck in shirt pockets for long days of riding, or to make a meal at home, or just to snack on. Umm good!

Yeast Bread

2 cups warm water
2 packages dry yeast
1/2 cup sugar
6 cups white flour
1/4 teaspoon salt
1 teaspoon baking powder
1/2 cup oil
1 egg

In a large bowl combine water, dry yeast and sugar. Mix in 2 cups flour, salt, and baking powder. Add oil and egg. Let rise 5 minutes then add 3-1/2 cups more flour. Sprinkle 1/2 cup flour on bread board. Knead dough. Let rise. Knead again then place in greased bowl and allow to rise, in a warm draft-free place. When dough has doubled in size knead and then fashion into buns or loaf pan. Place in greased cooking pans to rise until double. Bake about 25 minutes in 375° oven.

My neighbor on the Yolo Ranch helped me make this bread after she learned I was having a difficult time making yeast bread in the Canyon. Altitude makes a difference. And so do ovens. I was baking in a wood stove oven at the time. It was all a challenge but we won. This recipe is still my favorite and I always think about the late dear Pat Murphy every time I make it.

CHAPTER FOUR

Like Old Times

Bob and I dressed in western garb for our trip to Bagdad, the old mining town where our friends were working, Betty in the bank and Gene in the mine. I planned to call Mike and my parents from the pay phone at Kirkland Junction. We knew they all were waiting for more news from us; their plans hinged on the ranch deal.

We took the bumpy drive to Wagoner, eight miles away, where an abandoned board 'n batten post office and general store had been located. Our neighbor, Nel Cooper, had been postmaster there years before. I looked forward to visiting with her as I'd learned she had an interest in writing also and was up by 4:00 a.m. to work on her manuscripts before the day's ranch activities began.

At Kirkland Junction I dialed Mike's number in Missouri. "How's the roundup going?" he asked.

"Okay. . .a little slow. They haven't gathered many cattle yet but so far the Hereford cows look good. Calves too."

"How do you like the ranch?" he asked, eager for my impression.

"The range is very rough but I love it! The buildings are in good repair. We hope this deal goes through but there're a lot of details to work out yet."

After talking with my folks we drove to Hillside then took a winding mountain road leading to Bagdad, arriving mid-morning.

At the company store I purchased a large beef roast, bacon and eggs, and two fryers as well as several tins of corned beef. Bob wasn't much in favor of imported beef products, but I would have to use them to extend fresh meats until we could shop again. It wasn't at all handy but that was the way it was and I'd make do—there really wasn't any choice. We packed the meats in our large Coleman cooler-box, then drove to Betty and Gene's place.

"Come in to this house!" Betty exclaimed, grabbing me in a loving bear hug. Gene joined her at the door to welcome us, shaking hands with Bob and laughing in his deep good- natured voice. Memories of past years flooded over me and brought happy tears to my eyes. The Criners were like family, an important part of our lives.

"We'll take you for Mexican food for lunch," Betty said. "There's a new place open since you were here. We've been enjoying their food." (I seriously doubted any food could come close to her southern cooking, however.)

"How's the roundup coming along?" Gene asked Bob. "Not as wooly as those in Burro Creek, I wager."

"Wooly enough," Bob replied with a grin. Gene had helped on many of those hectic cattle drives.

"By the way, I was down there deer hunting a while back," Gene said.

"I hope the new owners are cleaning the cow trails of rocks and thinning out the brush thickets," Bob said. "The canyon will reclaim itself if they don't. Six years is a long time for nature."

"You folks worked at it all the time, I recall—even used a garden rake to clear out rocks on your road going up the mountain."

"That road!" Betty shuddered and laughed. She had driven it once on her way down to visit me. Most people were afraid of the steep road and few attempted to drive it.

Gene said, "How's Mike and his family? I'll bet he's looking forward to getting back here."

"He sure is, but it's going to be hard for Joyce Mae to leave Missouri and all her family. But Mike told her before they married he might want to return to Arizona ranchlife. I called them today. Baby Todd recognized my voice," I recalled happily.

"Betty, I've found a miner's dump close to the house. I got several old bottles for my collection. Bob says there's other dumps on the place and we can take the jeep and poke around."

"Sounds good to me!" Betty declared enthusiastically.

The day was wearing on. Roundup would resume early the next morning so we reluctantly left Betty and Gene shortly after our Mexican food lunch and started back to the ranch.

"Come see us soon," I called. I could hardly wait to begin storing new memories.

That night when we arrived home a semi-truck load of hay arrived for the roundup, and for several hours men walked past our house going over to Joe's place for coffee breaks, we assumed. It was impossible for me to sleep so I got up to re-read my newly written story. Bob was sleeping peacefully. Nothing much ever disturbed him; everything at all unusual did me. And a story often kept me awake with words going over and over in my mind; adding some, subtracting others until I'd finally get up to make the changes on paper.

Betty's Hawaiian Dressing

Blend:
    1/2 cup salad oil
    2 tablespoons vinegar

Add:
    1/3 cup catsup
    1/4 cup sugar
    1/2 teaspoon paprika
    1 small onion, chopped fine
    dash of salt

Store in refrigerator until used on vegetable salad.

CHAPTER FIVE

Cooper's Ranch

The Wagoner community was giving a surprise birthday party for Nel Cooper, and we were invited. While Bob was working cattle that morning, I washed and set my hair and baked a pineapple upside down cake for the two o'clock potluck. Bob arrived home late and exhausted so we canceled our plans to attend, until George and Joanie said they would drive us to the party. They urged us to go and meet our neighbors. I felt sorry for Bob. It had been a long day for him and he was still recovering from pneumonia, but he took a bath and stretched out on the bed to rest while I got ready.

When we arrived at Cooper's some of the guests were leaving to drive home to Prescott and Wickenburg, but there was still a good crowd and the table of food under the house veranda was abundant. I placed my cake on the long table.

George introduced us around, first to Nel, a widow of many years, then to her three sons Roy, Bob and John who helped run the ranch along with John's children, Mary and John Bill. Nel was a spry 72-year-old, witty and entertaining in spite of past hardships and years of ranch work. She had homesteaded part of the ranch back when they ran angora goats and employed Mexican herders. "They used to run goats on your place also," she informed us. "Get a plate and help yourself to the food," she invited.

Bob said, "Joyce's mother, Marge Williams, remembers meeting you at a woman's club in Prescott a few years ago. She and Earl will be living on the ranch. You and she should have a lot to visit about, and Joyce's son and his family will move out soon, too."

"A family ranch," Nel commented with a pleased expression.

We enjoyed visiting with everyone at the party, but George soon indicated it was time for us to leave. Roundup would continue the next day, bright and early.

Jay had been home seeing his family for two days, and when he returned to the ranch he brought Ruth and Lea, his wife and 13-year-old daughter with him for the weekend. He'd told us he might, so we'd put up a cot in the bunkhouse for Lea.

Early Saturday morning I put a large beef roast in the oven and would add carrots, onions and potatoes to simmer in the broth later. This menu would free me to visit with Jay's family, and perhaps take a hike with them to explore the area.

I was delighted to see them when they all arrived mid-morning. Ruth had thoughtfully brought a loaf of her homemade bread and a blackberry cobbler for lunch, which we would eat at the picnic table on the patio this beautiful fall day.

We were washing dishes after lunch when I said, "I've found several pretty little spots down the creek. Would you like to go there with me?"

Both women seemed agreeable to this suggestion and so we set out and walked as far as Logan's Arena.

"Isn't this a roping arena?" Lea asked when she saw the fenced area under the cottonwood trees.

"Yes. One of the cowboys that used to work here was a top-notch roper, we're told. He used to practice here."

Soon we noticed coon tracks by the little stream, prompting us to wonder if he had washed his food in the water, as is common practice with raccoons. Seeing the tracks prompted Ruth to mention the pet coon they'd had on a previous ranch, the one who'd stolen cigarettes out of Jay's pocket with such delight. I noted a sad wistful expression when she said, "It's too hard to part with pets when we leave a ranch." And I felt sure she was telling me that Lea and she wouldn't be moving to the Hozoni Ranch. We liked Jay. He was a good cowboy, but being separated from his family would be painful and if they couldn't be with him, he would eventually move on.

Shortly before George and his family moved, Joanie invited me to ride up with her to meet the school bus and get her kids. "You can meet Ruth Carter, the bus driver," she said. And so I went with her, driving two miles up our road to the bus stop to meet the friendly woman who had driven the bus for several years. In a few short years Todd would be riding that little yellow bus to the Walnut Grove Country School located 16 miles north. I felt sure he would be in capable hands.

Joanie was packing now. One day I baked an apple pie for their supper and also made a Red Hot Jell-O Salad, wanting to lighten her cooking a bit. She had been very considerate of me from the beginning. Several days later I walked through the empty house and discovered she'd left it in excellent condition. Even the many windows had been washed, inside and out. Mom and Dad's little house was left neat, too. We'd have nothing to do but move in when the van arrived with our Missouri furniture.

In the meantime, two cattle buyers arrived from Phoenix to inspect our sale cattle. They stayed for lunch. Bob always wanted me to cook a complete meal for cattle buyers—not just a sandwich and coffee. And three days later I fed four men when the livestock were finally loaded out—after the buyer's hot check had cleared the bank! That had involved two trips to Prescott to check on it.

All I can say about feeding extra men is I'm glad I was young and loved to cook. . . and I loved being a ranch wife.

A few days later those same cattle buyers sent two saddle horses up to the ranch for our approval. We hadn't purchased any horses with the ranch deal. These animals had been bought for resale. One was acceptable, but the second one had been eating loco weed, evidently, because he threw fits and tried to dislodge his rider. (Loco weed is a member of the pea family that cattle and horses will sometimes eat.) So back to Phoenix he went, and we were very thankful he hadn't hurt anyone!

Red Hot Jell-O Salad

1 package of strawberry Jell-O
1 cup red cinnamon candy
1 cup applesauce
1/4 cup chopped walnuts

Melt candy in 2 cups boiling water, stirring frequently. Add Jell-O. Stir in applesauce and walnuts. Refrigerate until set.

This recipe was given to me by Verbina Swearengin when we lived in the Ozark Mountains. She often served it with ham or pork chops and so do I.

Grandma's Apple Pie

6 tart apples, peeled
1 cup sugar
1 teaspoon cinnamon
1/4 teaspoon nutmeg dash of salt
1/4 cup butter

Slice apples into an 8-inch pastry shell. Sprinkle sugar, cinnamon and nutmeg over apples. Dot with butter. Top with crust, with sugar on top. Bake 60 minutes in 370-degree oven.

Grandma Williams taught me to make her apple pie, a favorite with the family and always on the menu for get-togethers. She used lard for the shortening, as was common before cholesterol worries. Later we used Crisco or other vegetable shortening.

In those days our pies were baked in a portable tin oven set over a kerosene stove burner to heat. The oven did a fine job of baking after one learned to adjust the flame.

Later I baked Grandma's Apple Pie in a wood cook-stove oven in Burro Creek which was another cooking adventure!

CHAPTER SIX

Drifting Cattle "Rep"

The tally was still very short. Joe sent word to several ranches that he wanted to ride their adjoining ranges in case any Hozoni cattle had drifted. Sending word was an old-time courtesy.

Then, one day we received a note in our mailbox from Nel saying some of the missing cattle had been spotted on the Cooper Ranch, so Bob sent Jay to help with their cattle work. Sending a 'rep' was another old custom.

Two days later I rode along with Bob to get the livestock they'd gathered in the big cattle truck we were purchasing in the ranch deal. This was Cooper's shipping day, a colorful scene with cowboys urging the cattle into the board corrals whistling and popping ropes against chaps, dogs barking. A short distance away, Nel had two cookfires going where two pots of pinto beans were bubbling. One pot was hot and spicy seasoned with chili peppers and cloves of garlic, the same as she'd prepared for Mexican cowboys in years past. The second pot of beans was milder for 'gringo' tastes. A large granite pot was full of boiled coffee for cowboys and guests. A long table constructed of planks lying on sawhorses held cups, paper plates, silverware and napkins, and a box of assorted donuts. Soon the mailman arrived to put mail in the long row of boxes, then he got out of his car and joined us at Nel's cook area. She introduced us to Herb, a friendly little man who was well liked we soon learned, and poured him a cup of java to go with a cake donut.

Later we returned to the ranch with four cows. Bob drove up to our corrals to unload them, and I decided to take my morning walk before lunch preparations. I'd developed the habit of taking a morning hike whenever possible. That day I decided to search for the old stage coach route hoping to find the tire tracks, which are sometimes visible for many years. And I did find them south of the stage stop: my curiosity about the building was increasing.

On the way home, I heard the faint sound of running water and was delighted to locate a small spring behind the second block house where my parents would live. . .if the ranch purchase was accomplished.

Wild mint was growing profusely along the stream. An old miner's gold pan lay near the spring. I wondered how much gold had been found there after creek risings, rushing through the mountains, picking up minerals along the way. More than one miner had made a modest living panning for gold on the Hozoni during the Great Depression. Some had stayed long enough to build cabins. Numerous rock chimneys and fireplaces remained in the area. Entire families had lived here also. A rope swing remained on a cottonwood tree limb, and riding toys were found in an old dump close to the house, providing proof of their, or other ranchers, presence. The spring was in a small shady area, inviting. I went there often in the days to come. A calming spot, an ideal place to regroup my thoughts and to settle ragged nerves when things went wrong on the ranch, as they sometimes do.

Tap, tap, tap, a red headed woodpecker was digging holes in a nearby tree searching for bugs. Then a small wren came to a brush thicket, landing quite close. He stayed to inspect me, cocking his head quizzically.

One morning, Joanie's three-year-old son Joe was waiting for me when I started on my walk. Without a word he started to join me. I asked, "Would you like to go with me on my walk?" He nodded and I said, "Go ask your Mama if you can." He darted to their house and came back all smiles.

Everyone said Little Joe was very quiet and didn't talk very much to anyone—only because he preferred not to, I soon discovered. He was chatty with me. When I asked him, "See the butterfly?" he commented, "We call them moths." It was indeed a moth and I was impressed with his identification of the large tan and brown moth.

We walked a short distance, then returned to the houses. I had welcomed his company. It reminded me of hikes taken with my young son when we were in Burro Creek Canyon, beginning when he was nine.

I enjoyed several more walks with my new little friend before he moved away from Peaceful Valley with his family. Soon my grandson would move here and before long he would be large enough to join me on nature hikes. . .it would be a magical time.

CHAPTER SEVEN

A Red-Letter Day

The cattle tally remained short after riding neighboring ranches and gathering a few head. And so the roundup continued. I hunkered down knowing we might be living in the little house for quite a spell yet. To pass the time, I washed the kitchen curtains and waxed the floor and took my morning hikes to settle my jittery nerves and quiet the uncertainty about our future should the ranch sale fall through, a frightening thought. We had been unsettled far too long. . .what would we do? We couldn't return to Missouri; Bob's health wouldn't permit that. Three cases of pneumonia had settled it once and for all.

But suddenly Bob decided to bring the roundup to a halt when he said, "Let's go to town and sign the sale papers, Joe." And so on October 20, 1970, Bob and I met with Joe, Lorraine, and their realtor in our attorney's office in Prescott to read the very long contract. It took several hours to complete and there were very tense moments over unclear wordings, namely how the cattle shortage would be handled. A price adjustment would need to be determined before the first ranch payment came due. Finally it was settled.

After supper Bob rented a motel room for the night as we both were exhausted and we had a long list of shopping to complete before returning to the ranch.

I made two brief calls to Missouri that night, saying, "We signed the papers today. It's a short escrow. See you soon!" I told Mom and Dad. I could hear sighs of relief on the other end and elation in Mike's voice. He would soon be coming home to Arizona ranchlife.

CHAPTER EIGHT

Welcome to the Hozoni

A recent letter from my parents stated their retirement home in Elkhead, Missouri had sold to a neighbor who greatly admired the free-standing fireplace Dad had built in the family room. Now Mom and Dad would be able to join us on the Hozoni!

A few days later, Bob and Jay were setting up a heating stove in their house when I commented, "Mom and Dad said they might arrive today if everything goes as planned." The mornings were getting chilly now and heat would be welcome, especially for Dad who had developed rheumatoid arthritis.

When my folks arrived that afternoon, it felt like it had been a very long time since I'd seen them. So much had happened since leaving Missouri, so much uncertainty over the ranch deal. I hugged them time and again. Dad looked tired after the trip, but they were excited over returning to Arizona and he was glad to be on a ranch again, recapturing his childhood days on the small family ranch in El Cajon Valley, California.

"We brought your mail," Mom said. 'We met a man named Roy Cooper. He showed us which box belongs to the ranch and he said a bookmobile will come to Wagoner next Friday about ten o'clock—that's a surprise!" she commented.

"We'll drive down, if we can," I promised.

"Roy said there's a good selection of books to choose from and we can check them out for a month," she said. Her face was radiant over this unexpected development, library books delivered from the Prescott Library stopping along the way to schools and stores. It was a service welcome to rural people. Mom enjoyed reading and had spent many hours doing so since her retirement from teaching. And she could socialize at the bookmobile too, which she loved doing.

"Bob and Jay are riding. There are still calves to brand," I said. "Come on in," I invited, showing them into our temporary home. "I'll put on the coffee pot." Dad's face lit up at the mention of coffee. "And I have a new recipe to go with it."

After several cups of java and warm coffee cake, we went out to their car to bring in suitcases and sacks of groceries. It all seemed familiar, like the old days when they would bring our mail to Burro Creek in a brown paper sack and special groceries—foods we all liked that were treats.

Everything was fitting in smoothly like pieces of a jigsaw puzzle. Tomorrow the van would arrive with all of our furniture.

Shortly after supper we heard the pilot car and large moving van creeping off the hill. The young driver looked weary. "We'll go back to Prescott for the night and unload in the morning," he said. Normally we would have asked them to spend the night on the ranch but every bed was occupied and I'll admit I was relieved not to have two extra men to cook for. . .I wanted time to catch up on family news.

The next day Mom and I were finishing breakfast dishes when the movers returned to unload our furniture. They asked me to stand out by the van and direct them to the correct house for the furniture. Mom was waiting in their home for heavy things to be put in the proper places, requiring little rearranging later. From time to time I went over to our house with furniture I'd planned for a specific spot.

Dad had given me their camel-back trunk and an antique rope bed for our large spare bedroom. (It had no springs, ropes replaced them.) The bed and trunk were attractive in there on the braided rug from our farm house. And Dad's antique guns,

Navajo rugs, and Indian artifacts fitted into their second bedroom beautifully.

The unloading continued all day. By late afternoon we were settled in, except for boxes of books and kitchen items.

The young men were tired, and so was I. They had done an excellent job. "Go get steak for supper," I suggested, handing them well-earned tips.

Later, when I walked through our house I was thrilled at how well the furniture fitted in and very glad we had brought everything. Every stick of furniture was needed in our home and up at the bunkhouse.

There was a feeling of fall in the air now. Nature was declaring it by a change of colors on the brush and trees, and by the animals' heavier coats, preparing them for cold winter days ahead.

Thanksgiving morning I went to the kitchen early to stuff the large turkey Dad had bought for the occasion, a beautiful plump bird. Between sips of my morning coffee I completed the project and popped the bird in the oven.

Bob soon arose and went into the living room to build a fire in the Franklin stove, the first since moving into our house. The aroma of wood fire drifted into the kitchen where I was working happily, reminding me of holidays on other ranches with family and friends. Having Mike and his family with us would have completed today's picture.

I hadn't hung curtains at any of the windows yet, but I arranged the beautiful handmade tablecloth on our long table overlooking the valley. Bob's mother had given it to him years before. She had made one for each of her seven children; also handmade quilts. Her handiwork always had a prominent place in our home.

Bob went out to feed the horses and milk cow while I arranged four place settings on the table. Soon there would be three more family members with us for holiday dinners and other guests too; sometimes a cowboy and his wife living in the bunkhouse would also join us. Today Bob had given Jay two days off and he had gone home to be with his family.

Our menu for that first Thanksgiving on the ranch was traditional: turkey and dressing, mashed potatoes and gravy, candied sweet potatoes, green beans seasoned with bacon, fruit salad and molded salad, homemade rolls, Grandma's brown bread, pumpkin and apple pie for dessert.

After dinner Bob set up our card table in the living room near the crackling fire and a game of cribbage began with a bet on who would win; losers would treat for lunch in Prescott at a later date.

At chore time we saw the remuda trailing past on the hillside behind the stage stop. Bob and Dad went to fill morrals while Mom and I set out lunch leftovers for our evening repast using paper plates for this meal. With the cooking behind us, this evening meal on holidays was always the most relaxed and enjoyable of the day.

Christmas preparations would begin by sending a box of gifts to Mike and his family. Maybe they would be with us next year if the Missouri farms sold.

Grandma's Brown Bread

Sift together:
    1-1/2 cups flour
    1-3/4 cups graham flour
    1/2 cup dark brown sugar
    2 teaspoons soda
    1 teaspoon baking powder dash of salt

Add:
    1 cup raisins

Combine:
    2 large eggs
    2 cups buttermilk
    1/2 cup molasses
    1/3 cup melted shortening

Add to flour mixture. Bake 50 minutes in two greased bread pans in 350-degree oven.

Coffee Cake

    1/2 cup white sugar
    1 egg
    1/2 cup whole milk
    2 tablespoons melted shortening
    1 cup white flour
    1/2 teaspoons salt
    2 teaspoons baking powder
    1 tablespoon vanilla

Topping:
    1/2 cup brown sugar
    2 teaspoons cinnamon
    2 tablespoons flour
    2 tablespoons melted butter

Cream sugar and egg together, add milk and shortening. Sift flour, salt and baking powder together and add to first mixture. Combine topping ingredients and spoon on cake. Bake about 25 minutes in a 350-degree oven.

CHAPTER NINE

Robert's Line Camp

On November 11, a load of our Charolais bulls arrived from Missouri at 8:30 in the morning. Bob and Doris Cooper, Nel's son and daughter-in-law, were in front of the truck showing the way to our ranch. The driver had stopped at Cooper's to ask for directions. I put on the coffee pot, of course, and the truck driver and Bob Cooper had a cup before going up to the corral to unload the bulls.

Later, Bob Cooper helped Jay and Bob brand the bulls with the ML ranch brand, running them through the cattle chute and heating the irons in the fire. We were thankful to have the chute. With so many large bulls to brand the chute lessened the work considerably. Heading and heeling them would have been burdensome even though both Bobs were outstanding ropers and had participated in rodeos for years.

Doris and I prepared lunch while the men were at the corral. About noon they came in and the five of us sat down to eat after filling our plates at the handy food bar. I loved this kitchen! Soon we would be eating holiday meals here. But in the meantime I would unpack clothes, more kitchen utensils, and my books in the den. I was pleased to have that special place for writing where I could leave an unfinished manuscript on the desk to return to another day—far better than the kitchen table where I'd always written before and had to remove my story before serving a meal.

I had submitted "A Horse of His Own" to a magazine where I'd been previously published but they returned it with this comment: "We are swamped with this type of material." At the time I was crushed but I now realize a large magazine has many submissions and a rejection is always possible, even after past sales there. I'd had three. On our next town trip I studied magazines on the newsstand and found a new one in print. So I sent them a fresh copy of my story hoping they hadn't been swamped with first horse stories. They hadn't and I sold it to them for more than the first magazine paid! So now I had two possible markets.

A few days later Bob asked me at breakfast, "Wanta go down and see the Robert's Line Camp with me? I need to put out salt blocks along the way and check windmills to see if they're pumping okay. (Salt was always put near water, either stream, tank or windmill.)

So we loaded up and Bob called his faithful cowdog, "Come on Sam, let's go!" I saw the old Catahoula following us in the side view mirror, panting and happy. He seldom left Bob's sight whether on horseback or in the truck. It had always been so ever since he was a pup and he started working cattle with Hanna, his mother. Sam's special attachment to Bob was why we'd moved him to the Ozarks with us six years before and back to Arizona later.

Our first stop was at a windmill and tank on the hill south of the house, then we continued down a long grade in our four-wheel drive truck, passing a side road going down to another windmill which was usually reached by Jeep, Bob told me. I later learned why.

The next road to the left took us into the Ward Line Camp where an ugly wood cabin stood on a hill. Below was a set of corrals and a holding pen. While Bob put out block salt near the tank I inspected the forlorn cabin. There was no evidence of it having been used recently. It seemed spooky for some reason. I never looked inside again and we never camped there although I sometimes cooked a meal outside over an open fire when the men were working in the corrals. I had no reason to dislike the place but two serious accidents later occurred there to Bob. Could I have somehow sensed they would happen?

Winding down the mountain we headed south toward the Robert's Line Camp. To my right I caught a glimpse of a windmill glistening in the early morning sun and a tin-roofed cabin situated in a grove of trees. When we arrived at the camp I hopped out of the truck to open a wire gate for Bob. He drove up to a stock pond to put out salt. Sam trotted behind to get a cool drink while I hurried down to the tin-sided cabin and swung open the door. The room showed a long vacancy. Dust was thick on the cooking pans that had been left on the drainboard along with a kerosene lamp. The food supply in the cupboard was nearly zero although camps are usually well stocked with staples should someone ride by and need a meal. Magazines and newspapers were strewn near a cot.

Outside a pile of junk established that someone had lived in the cabin for a long time. An outhouse had been built in a brushy area up the draw.

I heard running water and walked over to a small ravine about 50 feet away to investigate. There a stream was cascading over rocks in the small creek bed, feeding cottonwood trees along the way. A surprise in this semi-desert country. In the cottonwoods shading the corrals a pair of orioles was busily repairing the cone-shaped nest toward the coming season.

In spite of the disarray I liked this cabin; felt serene here—a sharp contrast to Ward Camp where I'd felt uneasy and eager to leave.

Bob poked his head in the doorway and said, "We'll get it cleaned up before spring branding. I'll need you to camp down here and cook for us." That comment pleased me. The cabin had possibilities and I'd welcome the quiet solitude while the men were rounding up and branding.

"Let's go home," he said to me. "Let's go, Sam," he called.

We left for headquarters, but I'd soon be back to this lovely spot with the singing birds and gurgling stream. I'd soon be back.

The Outhouse©
by Mike White

It's three in the morning
I feel the warning.

It's coming on slow
But I have to go.

The place I use is way out back
From house to house a well beaten track.

It's winter so I don't have to worry.
No snakes a-crawling or scorpions that scurry.

I step out the door and already know
The night has given me two feet of snow.

With long johns on and feet that are bare,
I bolster up the courage and charge out there.

A ring of frost around the seat.
This sure ain't going to be a treat.

But bold and brave I set on down
and with tears in my eyes I look around.

The toilet paper I hold so dear
Is frozen solid with ice so clear.

A Sears catalog with a page or two
I guess in a pinch will have to do.

Why did I cut that half-moon there?
I guess for something through which to stare.

But now the snow is blowing in.
Sometimes it seems you just can't win.

Well the deed is done. It's time to go
Back to the house through all that snow.

I start to get back to my feet
But my rear has frozen to the seat.

Thank God I didn't get around
To find the time to bolt it down.

The rest of the story I will not tell.
I'm sure that you can see it well.

I had no neighbor to see me and stare
At the toilet seat so stuck back there.

With stove so hot and butt so near,
The toilet seat I hold so dear
Was slowly melted off my rear.

Only then I realized with sorrow
I shore as hell won't ride tomorrow.

CHAPTER TEN

There's Work on the Hozoni

Shortly after Christmas, Jay was called home because of family illness, and he gave his notice to leave the ranch. We had enjoyed his stay with us, his pleasant ways and excellent help would be sorely missed.

Bob immediately drove down to Wickenburg and left word at the Saddle Shop that we needed a cowboy. And the next time we were in Prescott he went to the Palace Bar, saying there was work on the Hozoni Ranch. Bars and saddle shops were the traditional places to advertise for a cowboy, just as they and wagon yards had been in earlier days. But some men would stay on a ranch only a few days and then draw their pay. As Bob described it, "As soon as they got the wrinkles out of their bellies they'd be gone."

Bob was the boss of our outfit, hiring and firing as he felt necessary. Sometimes it was only a matter of economics and had nothing to do with the man. I as cook and bookkeeper had no part in the decision of who would go and who would stay. It became increasingly difficult for me to write that final check, especially when I didn't agree with Bob's decision. . .but a ranch can have only one boss.

In the old days wives who were known "whiners" or "agitators" were not welcome on a ranch because they kept their husbands stirred up and caused trouble. Sometimes a man would be told not to bring his wife with him, to find a place for her to stay in town. I don't know how it is these days though I suspect it's the same.

In late February we were sent a cowboy from Prescott. He and his woman were badly in need of a square meal and drinking money. They lasted only a few days.

Then two cowboys drove in our yard. I'll call them John and Jim. Both men came with good references, but we only needed one hand until roundup so Bob hired John for the spring branding, due to begin in March. He was to help with the ranch work, and Jim would attend to bunkhouse duties and occasionally ride horseback when needed.

I remember John was assigned to repairing pasture fences while Bob and I went to the Phoenix Livestock Auction, where Bob bought 150 head of crossbred cows and 42 calves to supplement the Hereford cattle purchased with the ranch. Bob had seen what crossbreds would do in rough country while ranching in Burro Creek Canyon, and he knew their calves would outweigh the Hereford calves by 50 to 75 pounds. More weight on the yearlings was needed to make our annual ranch payment.

The cattle were trucked up to the ranch where Bob, John and Jim rebranded them before driving them over the eastern side of the ranch to the old Miller Place, named after the homesteader who had once ranched there. That little outfit had been purchased years before by the Hozoni Ranch and was part of the ranch we had purchased.

Bob, John and Jim drove the cows over there to fresh grass. Mom, Dad and I drove behind in the truck, stopping in a shady spot under cottonwood trees for me to build a cookfire for the noon meal. It had been several years since I'd cooked outside and I recall being quite nervous over the possible results of the Dutch oven biscuits that Bob had requested I make. I built my fire and allowed it to die down to coals before I set the Dutch oven on to heat. After adding a tablespoon of shortening to the vessel, I spooned the biscuits into the grease, covered the oven with its lid and then shoveled hot coals on top, hoping it was the correct amount—if too much, burned biscuits might result! I surely didn't want that. But when I peeked inside the oven a few minutes later, I was relieved to find them browning nicely.

After lunch the men drove the cattle to a grazing spot where the grass was lush, having been left fallow for several weeks. Meanwhile, Mom and I cleaned off the dishes which we'd wash at home in hot, soapy water. Dad was searching for signs of a possible Indian camp, and found an arrowhead and numerous shards where it had been fashioned. It had been an interesting day and one I recall with pleasure.

CHAPTER ELEVEN

Kerosene Lamps

One morning in late February we awoke to silence. The diesel light plant had stopped running! Half asleep, I clicked on the bedroom light. "No lights," I announced to Bob. He took a flashlight and walked out to the stage stop where two kerosene lamps had been stored half full of kerosene. He brought them in the house and I lit the wick on one of the lamps. Immediately a cheerful glow filled the kitchen, reminding me of earlier days when we had lived in the canyon without electricity for years, but we were independent of it by using lanterns, a propane stove and refrigerator, and a gas-motored washing machine. But here everything depended upon the light plant.

I was enjoying the kerosene light and my recalls of those days until I turned on the water spigot in the kitchen and nothing came out. "No water, Bob," I said.

"I'll take a bucket up to the pump and get some. There's gravity flow from the storage tank on the hill," he replied.

While he was gone, I walked down to my folks' place in the early light. I could see a flashlight in their kitchen. "I brought you a kerosene lamp–the light plant has stopped. No water either. I guess you already know that. Bob is getting some for us. We'll need to ration until he gets the plant running."

"It's five degrees this morning," Bob announced when he arrived with the water. "No wonder the pipes are frozen up! Better get ready to go up to Skull Valley and buy a new fuse for the generator. I think that's what's wrong. They should have some at the general store. It'll save us driving all the way to Prescott."

"Do you need anything from the store?" I asked Mom when I told her where we were going.

"Yes! A loaf of white bread." she replied.

About an hour and a half later we arrived at the little town of Skull Valley, driving past the local café where several cars and trucks were parked, one with a horse patiently waiting in a horse trailer. Cowboys and locals were eating breakfast or having a coffee break. It was warm here in the lower elevation, and many ranches had begun branding or were just riding to check their cattle.

We drove up to the two-story store with living quarters above. The post office was located at the back of this building and several people were there reading their mail, sitting in comfortable chairs and on the built-in bench by the window.

Before driving home, we stopped at the café for hamburgers and coffee. Some old-timers were still visiting there. It was a friendly place, clean and inviting. And when the cook brought out a freshly baked peach pie, we had slices of that, too.

Then we started home. Bob would replace the fuse in the generator and we'd have power. But we didn't! That wasn't the problem, so Bob drove to the phone at Kirkland Junction and talked with a mechanic friend, asking him to come down to the ranch, which he did and we soon had electricity again. I wish I could say this was the only time we had to employ a mechanic but it wasn't, and we paid dearly for our modern convenience through the years in money and frustration.

CHAPTER TWELVE

Windmill Fizz

"Over yonder hill" was one of Bob's favorite directions. He might say, "Go get those cows over yonder hill," or "The line camp is over yonder hill," pointing in the general direction. I'd look in that direction and wonder which one of the hills was yonder? In time I learned to ask questions: To the right? How far? But only if it was imperative because Bob hated unnecessary questions. Old-time cowboys asked very few, he'd told me. Instead, they observed and learned from other hands. But I learned to ask questions after I'd taken several wrong turns or brought in the wrong cattle from "yonder hill."

It was one of those yonder hill directions that put me on a narrow jeep trail in our big ranch truck. I was on my way to the Ward Line Camp with Mom and Dad, planning to cook lunch for John, Jim and Bob as well as my parents. I'd been to the line camp once on the way to the Robert's Line Camp but I'd forgotten how far it was, and there were several side roads along the way. "Turn left," my cowman of few words had said. I failed to ask, "How far it is?" knowing he might say, "A fair piece."

And so I took the first left turn and began descending down a steep grade. The road narrowed. Nothing looked familiar. Too late I decided we were on the wrong road with no room to turn around and not a place to back up safely. By now the road was one that only a foolish nanny goat would have dared to travel! I had foolishly dared. We proceeded on down the hill and stopped at a windmill. It was pumping nicely, I noted.

Dad got out of the truck and helped me turn around by giving me hand directions, inching back and forth until the truck was safely headed in the right direction. Neither Mom nor Dad had said a word all during this experience, for which I was grateful.

When we reached the Ward Camp the cowboys were in with their cattle drive. Someone had built a cook fire and they were looking up the road with hungry, worried expressions.

"Did you have any trouble?" Bob asked me as I took my pots and pans out of the truck. "No. . . not much," I grinned at him. Bob would see my tire tracks on the way home. I felt sheepish over not taking better directions so I didn't report my detour in front of John and Jim.

Sure enough that night at home Bob casually remarked with twinkling eyes, "Someone's been down to the windmill."

"Yes, I know. Uh, the windmill is working real well," I reported.

He laughed and playfully tousled my hair. Only later did I learn my folks and I had taken a jeep road. Nothing larger had ever been used for driving down there, Bob informed me. I had become the first person to attempt it, giving me recognition I wasn't very proud or pleased with, and I still shudder at the recall!

CHAPTER THIRTEEN

Cowboy Castles

Bob poked his head inside the kitchen doorway where I was packing the box of camping groceries. "Are you ready to load up?" he asked.

"I think so. Hope I haven't forgotten anything!" I said as I checked my long list one last time. It was amazing how much needed to be packed for just three days at the line camp for only 9 or 10 meals but it still required many pots and pans, Dutch ovens and skillets, as well as groceries.

I hadn't camped out for seven years, ever since the last Burro Creek roundup before moving to Missouri. I'd forgotten how much stuff we'd always taken, first on a packmule and later in a truck after Bob built a road seven miles down to the camp; but I hadn't forgotten how much I loved to camp out! All the preparations seemed worth it, then and now.

"I'm ready!" I announced at last. Bob carried several boxes out to the truck and loaded them in back. I placed my sourdough jar on the seat beside me.

"See you in camp," Bob said. "We'll take the back trail and drive any cattle we find into the corral down there."

I watched John and Bob ride over the hill, old Sam trotting along behind, excited over the prospect of cow work.

I was excited too as I drove through the gate left open for me beside the barn. Getting out to close it, I then drove up to the horse pasture gate on the hill, getting out to open and close it behind me.

Taking a deep breath of balmy air, I sighed contentedly. As I drove south I noted several blue lupin and orange poppies dotting the hillside in this lower elevation. A roadrunner ran jauntily across in front of me; then a deer darted out of the brush and bounded across the hillside. A short distance away a ground squirrel scurried in front of the truck, his bushy tail held straight up, quivering nervously. In this area there was little to disturb the wildlife, and we would have ample opportunity to enjoy them in coming years.

When I arrived in camp, a pair of orange and black orioles was busy repairing their cone- shaped nest in a cottonwood tree shading the corral. Down the hill a short distance away was the line camp. The modest two-room tin building looked like a castle to me because it was quiet and secluded. In there I would be undisturbed and could pursue my writing while waiting for the cattle drives—sometimes for hours.

I parked the truck close to the cabin ready to unload. Getting out I poked around in back of the truck to find my coffee pot and container of ground coffee; I also unloaded the Dutch ovens ready for the noon meal. Next, I dug a small pit for the cookfire and arranged rocks around it, giving a place to set my cooking vessels after removing them from the fire. I raked around the cooking area and swept out the cabin before building a mesquite fire, my favorite wood for cooking. I collected extra wood while waiting for my coffee water to heat.

When I heard the windmill pumping I hurried to get water in a large bucket and a canteen from the pipe below the mill. Although someone had piped water down to the cabin in the past, the line was now rusty, requiring us to draw cooking and drinking water directly from the mill.

Hearing a small stream of water tinkling past the cabin, I stepped to the edge of the creek bank and stood listening as the water cascaded over the rocks. Noting the orioles still at work on their nest, I sat down on the bank to watch them and wait for the cow drive.

Just then I heard barking dogs urging cattle down the north trail, so I stepped inside the cabin so to be out of sight and not spook the herd. There I remained quietly while the cattle drank from the stream. It was a small drive with only a few young calves in the herd to brand.

In a few minutes the men urged the cows and calves into the corral, cowdogs yapping and nipping heels and working a little too eagerly until Bob called them off, "That's enough!" They went to him obediently, panting and wagging tails. They were having fun! I knew how they felt—it had been too long since we'd been on a Western cowdrive.

Bob and John unsaddled their horses to cool off their backs, and they ran to a sandy spot to roll in the dirt. Sam immediately went over to Bob's saddle and sat guarding it, as he always did.

The men unloaded my groceries and the heavy bedrolls, putting two of them on the iron cots in the small bedroom and one outside for John, which would give him a wonderful view of the stars.

Soon three thick steaks were sizzling in a covered Dutch oven and sliced potatoes were browning in a large frying pan. I peeked at my biscuits in the bread oven and was pleased with their progress, but the tops needed to brown a bit more so I shoveled additional hot coals on the lid, not too many, just a few.

Old-time chuckwagon cooks used one Dutch oven for frying meat or making stew and they reserved another oven just for baking breads, which they seldom washed, rather they wiped it clean with a rough rag which preserved the finish. Bob had taught me their methods of cooking, as he'd learned during his roundup days and long cattle drives.

At the end of our meal, I set out the tin of applesauce cookies I'd brought from home and I poured more coffee for everyone.

Long after the branding was done and I'd washed our dishes, I sat by the glowing embers of my cookfire, smelling the mesquite smoke, listening to a coyote's mournful howl, enjoying the moment. It was dusk now. Bob and John grained the horses from gunnysack morrals and then they slid into their bedrolls; soon I heard Bob snoring from our bedroom.

It was still dark when I woke the next morning. Someone had built my cookfire. Then I heard Bob in the feedroom at the back of the cabin filling the morrals. "Come on, boys," he called the horses. They nickered and trotted to him.

For breakfast I cut several thick slices of bacon off the big slab, then peeled three large potatoes ready for slicing and frying in the bacon drippings. Leftover biscuits from supper were cut in half, buttered and toasted in the bread oven, then I called "Chuck!" and poured three cups of freshly brewed coffee. Ahh good! Nothing like cowboy coffee on a crisp morning in cowcamp!

"We'll have stew and sourdough biscuits when you get in," I promised Bob. As soon as the men left I fed my jar of sourdough starter, adding some warm water, flour, and a little sugar to activate it, placing the jar near the warm coals to work. I loved cooking with sourdough—had since our Burro Creek days where I'd searched and searched for a recipe to make the old-time bread like Bob had eaten at the chuckwagons many years before.

That morning after cleaning up the dirty dishes, raking around the cooking area, and taking my morning sponge bath in a bucket of warm water I settled down to write the first draft of a camping story.

Each day cattle were gathered and brought in to brand the calves. On the fourth day we broke camp and loaded our truck to start home. Before leaving I walked over to the little stream to say goodbye, and to scatter bread and cookie crumbs under the cottonwood tree for the birds. It had been a magical three days, everything I'd hope it would be. This Cowboy Castle would always be special. And it was there I would write several stories for *Outdoor Arizona* and *The Western Horseman* and other publications.

Applesauce Cookies

2 cups sugar
1 cup shortening
3 eggs
2 cups applesauce
4 cups flour
2 tablespoons cinnamon
1/4 teaspoon nutmeg
1/4 teaspoon allspice
1-1/2 tablespoon warm water
1-1/2 teaspoon soda
walnuts or pecans, chopped
1 cup raisins

Cream together sugar and shortening; add eggs and applesauce. Mix well. Sift flour, cinnamon, nutmeg and allspice together into batter. Mix soda in 2-1/2 tablespoons warm water and add. Mix, then fold in raisins and nut meat. Bake on greased pan 12 minutes in 400-degree oven.

Biscuit Mix

4 cups white flour
2 tablespoons baking powder
1/2 teaspoon soda
1 teaspoon salt
4 teaspoons sugar
2/3 cup Crisco

Place in a quart jar. When ready to use, add 2 cups milk, preferably buttermilk, and 1 beaten egg. Knead lightly on floured board. Cut biscuits and place in greased baking pan, turning the biscuits over in the grease to coat the tops.

Bake 5 minutes in 450-degree oven, then 15 minutes longer in 425-degree oven.

CHAPTER FOURTEEN

Rabid Coyote

The day had started out so happily. I sang as I baked the chocolate cake and began packing food and dishes in the big cardboard box, never suspecting that the peaceful day would end in shock and confusion!

The spring morning was balmy and perfect when I loaded the things in the four-wheel drive truck, and checked to see if I had everything I needed for the cookout. The old granite coffee pot, a canteen of water, coffee, steaks, potatoes, homemade bread and butter, the cake—yes it was all there, so I set out toward the Ward Line Camp, four miles from headquarters where I was to meet Bob.

It didn't even bother me much when I managed to stick the truck in the loose, sandy wash about a mile from camp. The minute I felt it sink I shut off the motor and climbed out to size up the situation.

Not too bad, I thought, as I removed the shovel from the side of the truck, where we always carried it, and began shoveling the sand away from the wheels. Then I worked two gunny sacks under the front wheels as far as I could, shifted into low-low, and started the motor. Sure enough, the truck crawled across the sacks, out onto firmer sand and kept right on going. Once again I was on my way with lunch for the cowboys.

When I drove up to the camp not a cow was in sight—nor could I hear any sounds of cattle, cowdogs or cowboys. That meant I had some time to meander over the hillside close by, but first I collected firewood and stacked it ready to light, as soon as Bob and our hired cowboy corralled the livestock.

About an hour later I heard the cattle bawling, and soon the men and our five cowdogs had corralled them. I lit the fire and boiled the coffee. While I fried the steaks and potatoes, the fellows rested in the shade, drinking hot coffee and talking about the cattle drive of the morning.

It is rough, brushy country there on the lower part of the ranch. Unfortunately, some ornery cattle had given the cowboys the slip. Bob—never one to allow a cow to get away for long—decided to make a second cattle drive in hopes of gathering them. The men would be gone two or three hours, so after they left I set out afoot to explore some more of our new ranch. Much later, I sat down under a mesquite tree to rest. And when I heard the cattle bawling in the arroyo about one-half mile away, I thought, They're having trouble. I began to hear the dogs barking, then Bob began shouting. Never would I have suspected how much trouble they were having, for that is when they first encountered the coyote! He was wandering aimlessly, attacking anything that moved. Still oblivious to any possible danger, I ambled down to the truck and got inside—so I'd be out of sight when the cattle reached the corral gate. And when the coyote trotted alongside the truck and halted near a bush about 30 feet away. I wasn't concerned. But I should have realized he was sick when he paid no attention to the truck or the bawling herd. By nature a coyote is a shy, cautious animal, very alert to strange objects or sounds. Finally, he trotted over the hill without bothering to look back, though coyotes nearly always halt to look back over their shoulders.

Seconds later my husband galloped up to the truck and asked, "Have you seen a coyote? He's rabid!"

"Yes! Right over there!" I pointed to the right.

"He bit four of the dogs! Give me the Winchester! Here, hold my horse!" he shouted in rapid-fire succession. Then he said,

"Stay in the truck," as he handed me his horse's reins through the window.

Of course, Bob should have stayed on the horse, but he hadn't ridden him many times, nor had he shot from him. Actually one might have thought Bob was protected with his boots and heavy leather chaps as he walked up the road searching for a glimpse of the sick animal in the thick brush that covers the hillsides.

But the coyote had hidden somewhere to the left of the trail, for without warning he ran and leaped on Bob from behind, sinking his teeth in my husband's right hip—just above the chap belt! There the coyote clung trembling. Bob grabbed the coyote by the back of the neck with his right hand, forcibly removed him, and thrust him to the ground. The rifle was still in Bob's hand, but a bullet could have ricocheted off a rock at that close range. So he laid his gun down. He was stunned and unsure if the bite had drawn blood, as one often is when injured. His first thought was to choke his attacker, but he feared being scratched, which would require anti-rabies treatment the same as a bite. He had to kill this coyote! In desperation, he put one foot on the kicking, squirming coyote's neck and feverishly stomped his head. But the force of Bob's kick knocked the coyote's head right out from under his foot. Leaping up, the coyote darted away.

Bob grabbed his rifle and fired.

I heard cussing, then the loud report of three rapid shots. Suddenly, I was clammy cold and sick with fear. When Bob walked over the hill and down the road, the shock and horror of his experience was written on his face. Already, I was out of the truck when he exposed his hip, saying, "Did he get me?" It was a hard question to answer, though he took it calmly. I shall never forget the sight of the ugly wound, the teeth marks with their bloody declaration. It will be etched on my memory forever. Now he would have to take the dreaded rabies shots.

Yet, in spite of his ordeal, he insisted on riding to hunt for the animal which his three bullets had missed. Armed with the 30-30 and a pistol, the men rode searching for more than an hour.

As I waited in the truck, I saw the dreaded coyote come down the same road my husband had earlier walked up. Frantically, I honked the horn to signal the men—the coyote was completely oblivious to it. Then, before my eyes I saw the last of our cowdogs being bitten. He had been napping under a mesquite and when the coyote trotted down the road the dog jumped up, startled. The coyote ran over to him and savagely bit him several times around the head. Seconds later the men arrived, but the hunted animal had disappeared from sight into the brush, as in a nightmare. Again, the cowboys rode searching while I sat numbly in the truck.

Finally, I convinced my hot, tired man to call off the search and go to the doctor, but first he opened the corral gate and scattered the cows, with their unbranded calves, then he drove the four saddle horses toward home and into a somewhat safer area.

The four-mile ride home seemed endless. Our cowboy "rode shotgun" from the top of the truck, but he saw no sign of the rabid animal. When we reached headquarters I was still numb with the shock and dread for Bob. I do remember very vividly that my parents had read about the new vaccine which has fewer reactions. Quietly, they helped us prepare for our town trip.

Bob and I took hot baths with Purex in the water (two of the frightened dogs had jumped into the truck with me, hence my Purex bath), packed a bag for one night—or several—and at last we were on our way, 60 longs miles which would take nearly two hours to travel. We had discussed taking the dogs to town for confinement—but what if one should get away from us on the road. It was decided that we should pen them up, separately, until we talked to our veterinarian and someone from the sheriff's department.

In Prescott, our family doctor and the nurses at the emergency room in the hospital were very thoughtful of us. Then, after cleansing the wound, Bob received the first shot in the abdomen, which he stated was not as painful as he had expected. After resting 45 minutes to be certain he had no reaction, we left the hospital. It was then 10:30 p.m.

We rented a motel room and tried to sleep, but the questions spun crazily in our tired minds. Would Bob develop a reaction later? Would the cowdogs have to be done away with? (They had previously received rabies shots, but according to our vet, the vaccine is not 100 percent sure—especially if it is nearing the end of its protection. So, they were to be revaccinated and kept under confinement for five weeks.)

Would any cattle be bitten before the rabid coyote died, or was killed? Our cowboy was to return to the area where the coyote was seen—maybe he would shoot him. The hopes, the questions, were endless. At dawn we slept.

In his years of ranching, Bob had killed many rabid animals. Generally, they were in the final stages of the disease and were thin, coarse-haired; often with the blind staggers, sometimes slobbering. But the coyote that attacked him showed only the early symptoms—abnormal aggression.

"A normal coyote will turn a flip getting out of the way from a human," stated an avid outdoorsman. The vet and a trapper expressed similar opinions, thus confirming our belief.

Through study and talks with our doctor, veterinarian and trapper, we learned more about rabies. Though it is more prevalent in the summer months or during a drought, rabies may appear at any time of the year. In the early stages a rabid animal may not seem sick. He may not froth at the mouth. Frothing is sometimes noted in the final stage, just before death; however, he may never have this symptom. So beware of wild animals that have no fear of man.

So, each night at about 7:30 for the next thirteen days Bob received a shot. At the end of the series he had two boosters, one on the tenth day, another on the twentieth day—and it was over! We celebrated at our favorite restaurant, the Pine Cone Inn where Bob had proposed to me 14 years before, while a woman at the next table had smiled when she heard my reply. We ate dinner by candlelight while piano music filled the air; thankfulness filled our hearts. We thanked medical science, for thanks to it our story had a happy ending.

The next morning we returned home and discovered John and Jim's truck was gone and their camper shell was hidden in back of the bunkhouse. To change the description, perhaps? I soon discovered the bunkhouse was a mess! They had left in a hurry, leaving dirty laundry on the living room floor!

So Bob and I were stuck with morning and night chores before making the long trip to the hospital for his treatment.

The following day I made a cardboard sign, posting a warning on the road, saying: "Beware! Rabies in area."

Bob said, "Write Fran and Charles and see if they want a job." They had visited us on the Missouri farm to inquire about a job there. Perhaps they would want a job on the Hozoni. Their reply was prompt. They did! We could expect them in a few days.

CHAPTER FIFTEEN

Fran and Charles

Mom and I cleaned up the messy bunk house in preparation for the Penningtons' arrival; also made colorful cotton slipcovers for the backs of the worn kitchen chairs. In town Bob and I purchased a small wood stove for the living area to supplement the gas one in the bathroom.

Bob and I continued pouring out feed in the long wooden trough for the horses and driving around the dry range to detect any signs of illness. It was a depressing experience as we were in the middle of another Arizona drought with extra work and expense.

A few days later Fran and Charles arrived in their truck, pulling a trailer with Fran's barrel racing horse and the orphaned pet squirrels she had tamed. Fran would be riding the range with Charles and going to Phoenix with him for feed.

During the time they were with us I learned Fran had a special way with animals and I spent many pleasant hours at the bunkhouse learning about the animal friends she had nursed back to health in Missouri. I loved to hear about her patients. A special friendship was born over cups of coffee and freshly baked bar cookies.

Both Fran and Charles were (are) talented horsemen and Charles soon had Sourdough willing to go past the bunkhouse without bucking, a naughty habit he had acquired in earlier days and one he appeared to enjoy. No one had corrected this until now. Some people have a way with animals and they want to please.

As long as she can remember Fran has loved baby animals and being a foster mother to them. She cared for orphaned rabbits, squirrels, and ducks. She had nursed an injured chipmunk back to health; she had operated on and saved the life of an owl with a broken, infected wing.

She talked a bounty hunter into giving her a young fox. She even befriended four baby skunks—with no angry reactions!

To feed the little animals she wrapped them in a warm cloth with only the head out. Fran told me rabbits like to feed upside down the first week and cottontails are very hard to raise.

They must be fed from a bottle twice during the night; older rabbits will drink from a saucer like a kitten.

When a young deer was injured by a car Fran called the Fish and Game Department to report her having it. They suggested she put the animal down but Fran was able to nurse it back to health, probably due to her dedication.

It was a sad day for me when Fran and Charles drove away from the ranch a year later, after Mike and his friend David, who had been helping on the farm, arrived. We had too many cowboys and too little money to keep them all. Before they left Fran gave us a pair of bull horns for our living room wall. I have that gift here in New Mexico, a happy reminder of our days shared on the Hozoni. We have stayed in touch and recently Fran surprised me with a telephone call from their Missouri farm. She and Charles had been reminiscing about the ranch and had decided to call. Of course, I asked about her animal friends and learned she has befriended two flying squirrels that she keeps in the attic during cold weather. And she has two pet coons trained to the lease. She takes them for walks for exercise.

Some people have a special way with animals. We were fortunate to have Fran and Charles all those years ago, and our animals were mighty fortunate, too.

CHAPTER SIXTEEN

Relics of the Past

One morning shortly after our rabid coyote ordeal a member of the Desert Caballeros from Wickenburg came by the ranch to ask permission for their riders to cross our outfit on the way to Cooper's Ranch where they would camp for several days. There would be over 200 horseback riders from several states for this 26th annual ride. They hoped their catered food wagons could park on a large flat east of our house for lunch. And on their way out they wanted to view Dad's spur collection. Our neighbor, Roy Cooper, was a member of the Desert Caballeros which had been organized in 1947, and he suggested the men see the spurs after he'd viewed them several days before because he was impressed with the collection of relics from the past that Dad had collected for many years.

Bob and Dad received an invitation to join the riders for lunch at the wagon; also to spend the day in camp at Cooper's Ranch the following day where numerous interesting activities were planned. (No women ever attended these events, nor were they to be in sight when the riders went through, Roy informed us.)

There was a beehive of activity around headquarters as the day approached for our guests to arrive–raking, cleaning Mike's empty house, where the collection would be displayed, and arranging Dad's spurs and relics using Navajo rugs, Mexican serapes and natural-color burlap for the backgrounds.

Early on the designated day the catered food wagons rumbled past headquarters while I watched from the studio window. Excitement built. Later, Mom and I spent considerable time dashing outside to scan the southern hillside for the riders. She was the first to spot them. "There they come!" she exclaimed. It was an impressive sight seeing so many well-mounted riders winding their way down the trail. And then we hurried inside to alert Dad.

Later, Bob was all smiles when he came down from the lunch wagon. "The cook sent this to you," he said, handing me a warm package. I peeked inside and found a broiled beef patty with a slice of bacon wrapped around it, the same as the men had enjoyed for their lunch. I was pleased with his thoughtfulness.

"Did you see Dick Spencer?" I inquired about my editor at The Western Horseman. "Roy said he might be on the ride."

"Yep," Bob said. "I talked with him. He remembers your stories." A busy man like that—I could hardly believe it!

Now, men were emerging from the house next door having seen Dad's collection. The first spur Dad bought cost twenty-five cents at a blacksmith shop in Lakeside, California.

While pairs were always a welcome find, Dad was just as pleased with a single spur if it illustrated a time or place. He studied articles and framed a chart from the September, 1952 issue of Arizona Highways that showed the development of spurs during the centuries, beginning in 200 B.C.

It is interesting to note that some riders preferred to wear only one spur. General Sherman was such a rider, according to Daniel Oakey in his book Marching through Georgia and the Carolinas, where Oakey stated Sherman generally wore low shoes and one spur. And according to history, French cowboys wore only one spur, too, while in Argentina the gauchos wore two spurs—on their bare feet!

The 16th century Spanish-type spurs in Dad's collection were obtained in Mexico by a visiting archaeologist friend. Those spurs, with their six points and six-inch rowels always caused the most comments. It is said that the conquistador mounted his horse, then a servant strapped the spurs on the rider's boots. After lifting those heavy spurs, one believes it.

Later that afternoon there was a knock on our front door and there stood my editor, tall, handsome and smiling. Unbeknownst to me Dad had sent him over by saying, "There's someone next door who would like to meet you."

I had met the man who had accepted my first story to publish in The Western Horseman, after years of submissions to other magazines, and numerous rejections. Their acceptance had been very special when it had arrived in Missouri, shortly before our move to the Hozoni. And now, after all those years, I can still feel that tingle of surprise and pleasure.

The barn, corrals, saddle room, garage and blacksmith shop on the Hozoni.

The main ranch house.

Bob White

Joyce White

Betty Criner

Gene Criner

This is the spooky old Burro Creek Canyon Road
that Bob built.

Nel Cooper

Above: Nel and Roy Cooper
Below: Robert's Line Camp

Bob saddling Steamboat as Sam watches.

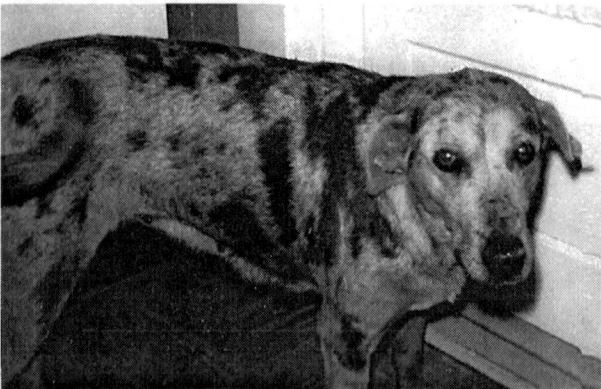

Hanna

Bob working the squeeze chute with branding iron.

Ward Line Camp.

First roundup on the Hozoni, 1970.

Cold with Morrel feed sack.

Fran Pennington at the water tank with Kansas.

Charles Pennington riding Kansas and leading the
packmule, Hollyhock, loaded with four salt blocks
for the water tanks.

The bunkhouse where Charles and Fran lived.

The lions grew big as they feasted on our cattle

Charles, Fran, Joe Caldwell - the Lion Hunter, and Bob.

Desert Caballeros 26th Annual Ride with over 200 riders.

Dad and I pictured with part of his spur collection.

CHAPTER SEVENTEEN
Preparing for Roundup

Two weeks after the Desert Caballeros riders came through the ranch the Las Damas obtained permission for their riding group from Wickenburg to come through the ranch and stop to see Dad's spur collection too. I remember standing outside that spring morning to greet the women and point them to the house where the spurs were still on display. Forty-two riders from Arizona and five other states signed my guest book and took photos of the collection that day.

We were preparing for roundup again, having stopped five weeks during Bob's rabid coyote ordeal. Now we were about ready. I'd lugged out my little chuckbox and cleaned it up, ready to haul it to the Robert's Line Camp where it would serve as my cupboard and work counter. And I gave the Dutch ovens and big granite coffee pot a good scouring, too. Then I prepared several quart jars of biscuit mix and poured my sourdough starter to work in a large mason jar.

It's lots of work getting ready for roundup and much of it begins three or four weeks ahead. Windmills are checked to see that they are working, and salt blocks are placed near every watering. Fences are ridden and repaired to hold cattle. Windmills were checked—17 of them—to see if they were pumping smoothly. It sometimes required new leathers in addition to oiling. The men had found the windmill up the draw close to the house needed attention. "Pulling a windmill" is the term the cowboys use. It requires a block and tackle to get the job done.

Mike was up on the windmill tower, 20 feet in the air. Loyd, our hired help, was pulling the rope. Suddenly it broke! The block fell, hitting Mike on his head, cutting a one-inch hole in his felt hat and two inches in his scalp which required 12 stitches to close. When the doctor saw the injury he remarked, " I don't know why you didn't pass out," to which Mike replied, " I couldn't, Doc—I was too high off the ground!"

The resting horses are brought in from the range, still a bit shaggy in their winter coats. Each one gets new shoes though some protest! They are grained morning and night, and are ridden on several short jaunts to toughen them up for the long distances they will carry the cowboys.

The men butchered a beef so I'll have meat to cook out on the range and at the line camp, as well as at home. I usually prepared a big kettle of Son-Of-A-Gun Stew the day of butchering and bake a pan of biscuits to go with it. In the freezer go pies, cakes, cookies, homemade bread and buns, all ready for the long days ahead. (I can only hope no one begins sampling beforehand!) Meanwhile, the cowpokes clean and oil their gear and ready their bedrolls. Boots go in to the cobbler, the wash is done. It's a busy, fascinating, and tiring time of the year.

I'd like to recall those roundups once again. Come on along with me.

The alarm sounds off at 5:00 a.m. We head to the kitchen for that first cup of cowboy coffee (boiled). Soon bacon and hot cakes sizzle and brown on the griddle, then I ring the old dinner bell to announce breakfast. Directly, the sounds of clinking spurs and saddling up in the early morning light are heard while cowdogs romp and bark happily. The spring work has begun!

We'll take lunches to the cowboys, and cook outside at various spots on the ranch where the men will be branding.

Sometimes we'll drive there in the jeep; more often we'll go in the four-wheel drive truck. Later on we'll camp a week or so at the line camp, a spot I dearly love, and several weeks later, when the sale cattle are gathered, we'll ship to market or show them to buyers here. The livestock inspector will arrive; coffee will be served around the long kitchen table. We'll hear news of other ranches and we're proud of our yearlings, the best he's inspected, he comments. Cross-breeding has paid off for us again.

But today our job is to take lunch to the Ward Corral, where Bob was bitten by the rabid coyote. We will be careful, but no sign of illness has appeared since that frightening day. We pack up the grub, a canteen of water, and a shovel. Pup, the youngest member of our cowdog crew, wants to ride along. I'll just shove him over a bit, and we'll be on our way, driving nearly an hour over a narrow mountain road.

By now it's 9:30, but the air is still crisp and invigorating. Up, over, around the mountains we bump, rock, and jounce. Soon we pass a windmill where a bunch of crossbred cattle are watering. Pup pricks up his ears and lets out a shrill little bark.

Roaring through the sand creek bed and winding through the canyon, we arrive at the Ward Camp well before the cattle drive. There's not a cow in sight. We drive some distance past the corral, so as not to spook the cattle when they come in. We sit in the truck waiting.

Soon we hear a deep-throated bawl, then another, and another. Pup perks up his ears and whines. Now cows and calves call back and forth as cattle are added to the holding bunch, grouped a mile or so distant. Even though they are far off, we can hear the cattle, dogs and cowboys, for the mountains surrounding that canyon hold in the sounds.

At last the cattle are corralled and a branding fire is built. Bob takes down his rope and builds a loop. Cowboys tuck piggin' strings (short ropes) in belts and stand ready to flank calves. Soon our ML brand will be on the calves.

Down through the years branding has been the traditional method of showing livestock ownership. Branding customs and history are fascinating and I found Irons in the Fire by Oren Arnold very good reading. He states that Indians used hot rocks to brand domesticated wild animals. (And wife branding was common in some tribes, too, as was self-branding for religious rites.)

Some of the old Spanish brands show a religious influence. Three Crosses, the brand of Hernando Cortez, is one. Thousands of brands were developed and it was necessary to have a record of them so that they would not conflict with neighbors' cattle.

Various methods of recording were used. In Mexico, the brand was sometimes burned on a piece of wood and kept on file. In Arizona, the rancher's brand was burned on a piece of rawhide and strung on a string, along with other ranch brands. But soon there were too many hunks of hide dangling on strings to keep track of the brands easily, so county brand books were compiled. And later a state brand book was printed.

Bob and I had the pleasure of seeing one of those early brand books at the Necktie Ranch in Walnut Grove in the 1970s. The leather-bound 1885 book contains 71 county brands, many of them initials such as our neighbor's NEL brand, belonging to Nel Cooper.

The Sharlot Hall Museum in Prescott has some of the original pieces of hide with early brands burned on them. And while doing research in old newspapers there, I came across the legal notices of ranchers who had recorded their livestock brands long ago.

Our Hozoni Ranch branding would continue for several weeks. Lots of meals would be served outdoors, and there would be many days of long, hard labor for cowboys, cowdogs, and horses. But we loved that way of life. It is said that Nevada, Arizona and New Mexico are among the last places where some things are still done in the old way: headin' and heelin' calves, branding from an open fire, sending a rep to help your neighbor. I was happy to have been a part of it.

Son-of-a-Gun Stew

I always made this old-time dish the day after we had butchered a young beef. Some cooks don't brown the meat or add onions; others do, and also add chili powder. There are several ways to make it.

Cut up the following meat:
   1 lb. heart
   1 lb. brisket
   2 sweetbreads
   1 lb. liver
   2 or 3 feet of tripa de leche (marrow gut)

Yes, I had a hard time forcing myself to work with this last ingredient the first time. In fact, Bob helped me through the ordeal—but one taste of the finished dish convinced me, because it is very delicious.

Salt, pepper and flour the meat and brown it lightly in hot bacon grease. Then add a large onion, chopped fine. Cover with hot water and simmer several hours until tender, adding water as needed. A Dutch oven is ideal for preparing this stew. Hot biscuits, a crisp salad, and plenty of coffee go with it nicely.

CHAPTER EIGHTEEN

A Surprise Visit

We were cutting and wrapping a hind-quarter of beef to put in the freezer toward roundup when we heard a car horn. Bob and I exchanged bewildered glances, then at the same time it dawned on us who it was. "It's Mike and Joyce Mae," I shouted, dashing outside.

They'd planned to visit us and see the ranch but no definite date had been set, just whenever the Missouri farm had a slight lull, and when Mike's friend David could tend the cattle for two weeks.

I brushed happy tears from my cheeks and looked at my loved ones, giving each one a big bear hug. How much Todd had grown! It had been seven months since we'd seen him. Would he remember us? I said the familiar words that I'd always used on the telephone to him, "Hi, Todd. What doing?" and his face broke into a wide smile.

Now Mom and Dad were hurrying out of their house to hug loved ones, laughing through misty eyes. I went to my kitchen and put on the coffee pot, then we settled down to catch up on news. Todd hurried to the chest where his toys had always been stored for him. Sure enough, they were still there! Now his smile widened, looking from face to face before settling down to play contentedly.

Mike had many things he wanted to do during their visit. And one thing was to spend a day in Burro Creek Canyon, a long talked about visit. He wanted Joyce Mae and Todd to see the place where he had grown up, and they invited me to go with them. Bob elected to stay home.

He had no desire to go back.

I was up at 4:30 the morning of our trip, packing lunches, pouring coffee in a thermos, setting out my camera and film. . .fidgeting. I was wildly excited! I had daydreamed of the day I would see my beloved canyon again, but I was frightened, too. Would it be as beautiful as my recall? Was I making a mistake in returning? Advice was strong against my going back—but I had to return, was almost ill with the need.

And so we piled into the four-wheel drive Ford and started out for Burro Creek. It was good we had an early start because it took considerably longer than we'd planned. When we reached Strotjost Flat the mesa was boggy due to a recent rain and we decided not to risk crossing it and the possibility of getting stuck. That cancelled our plan to drive to the canyon rim and look off into the beautiful valley. My heart sank with disappointment.

But Mike had another idea: We would drive a back road to Bagdad, then take a newer mine road into lower Burro Creek. Fortunately, Mike had taken an extra barrel of gas along.

The new road was steep and narrow, requiring several switchbacks. A spooky experience! But we arrived safely and not too far from the one-room line camp we'd built only eleven years before (It seemed much longer since I'd printed "Whites 1960" in the soft cement floor.) It felt unreal to be here again, almost dream-like.

I swung open the wide wooden door to look inside. The room was as we'd left it: time had stood still. The handy chuckbox Dad had built for us was still sitting in the corner, partly stocked with groceries. The small cast-iron stove was still there. The double bed and mattress was still there, ready to rest tired bones from the day's roundup. I recalled that Mike had always wanted to sleep outside in his bedroll so he could enjoy the blanket of stars twinkling overhead. Several cowdogs would keep him company and one or more would snuggle close. Suddenly I began laughing when I remembered Bingo and how the old cowdog had crawled under the bed, as he did at home on the screened porch, and now was declaring his camping domain. Once after gathering cattle in this lower country he hadn't wanted to leave camp and had stayed behind snoozing under the trees when we rode off, finally arriving home at chore time. There's something very special about camp life.

We were pleased to find the drought-resistant grasses we'd planted had multiplied and survived. But some cow trails were nearly full of rocks; brush was beginning to overgrow other trails. Nature was beginning to reclaim the land.

We ate our lunch in the shade of the cottonwood trees, Todd sitting in the wheelbarrow we'd used to mix the cement for the cabin floor all those years before.

We started back to our Hozoni Ranch shortly after lunch. I left feeling satisfied and complete and I'll always be glad I returned to the canyon that day. It hadn't been a mistake.

On the way home we stopped in Bagdad to see our dear friends the Criners, a brief stop as it was 5:30 by then and we had a long drive ahead of us. My folks and Bob would be waiting. We didn't want to worry them. It would be good to report that Bob's experimental grasses had multiplied and were hardy; that much of his years of hard work still showed and the ranch was still called 'The Bob White Place.'

I should update you about the old roads going into the canyon. All have been blocked to vehicles by rock slides. Now access only by horseback is possible. Part of the southern range was declared a wilderness area several years ago.

The current rancher and his family love Burro Creek Canyon as Mike and I did. . .and still do.

CHAPTER NINETEEN

Old-Time Corrals

Starting out on a shoestring, as many ranchers have done, sure makes a fellow resourceful! It seems that a lack of money puts the head to working, for the old-timers certainly knew how to use materials they had on hand. Take cattle and corrals, for example. In Arizona many types of old ones can be seen, and nearly all of them were built from what Nature gave the cowboy to work with. Rocks, trees, ocotillo, and even canyon bluffs were used as materials for corrals, as well as the usual wire ones with numerous staves.

On the Hozoni the cowboys were repairing several old wire corrals on the range before fall branding began. I went with Bob and our hired cowboy one day while they cut and trimmed the desert willow limbs that would be used for the repairs. And while I loaded the somewhat crooked branches that would dry into hard, long-lasting staves, I recalled some of the corrals we had worked in, and how skillfully the old-timers had used the available materials to construct them.

On our Burro Creek Canyon Ranch many types of old corrals were used. Long ago, horses had been wintered in the warm lower creek area, and a brush corral had been built that would hold 15 to 20 head of horses. The brush was piled about three feet thick and five feet high. One post had been set in the ground, and from it a wire gate was strung over to a mesquite tree. Only the wire had cost the builder any money, but the rest of the enclosure had involved many hours of labor.

Near our home in the canyon an early homesteader had built a rock corral. Later, one side was replaced with heavy poles and a wooden gate. By looking at it, one wouldn't think an animal could get out of that corral, but I remember one time when a determined, and very wild yearling circled it at top speed, sized up the situation and then nimbly climbed over the rocks. His dash to freedom was swift and complete up the dusty mountain trail.

Our favorite set of wire corrals was located near the creek about a mile from home. Cattle were easy to pen there, and the large sycamore trees offered a dandy refuge, should the case require. Bob enjoyed teasing me about the time we were branding calves and an enraged mother cow chased me—I ran past the trees and scrambled over the wire fence—with only seconds to spare. He remarked, "You're the only person I know who will run right past two safe trees!" (Nothing short of <u>outside</u> the corral looked safe to me at times like that!)

Myself, I recommend pole corrals—they are easier to climb. And just how easy depends upon the speed of the cow chasing you! I recall that Bob once broke the record for the ten-yard dash when a trusty old snubbing post came out of the ground, and the irate steer that was tied to it took after Bob—snubbing post and all! When the dust cleared, Bob sat with his knees tucked up under his chin, laughing. Below, the snuffy yearling repeatedly tried to hook him. By this time I was outside the corral—but I had a real good view of the action while peeking between the poles.

On the eastern edge of our new ranch Fran and Charles discovered the remains of two ocotillo corrals. The tall stems of the spiny desert shrubs were cut and placed in the ground to form solid walls; then they were tied together with baling wire. A wire gate was built across the opening and reinforced with more ocotillo stems. They had taken root and were leafed out—a pretty sight—but I couldn't imagine scrambling over those barbed limbs, can you? Still, ocotillo were plentiful and some old-time cowboy needed a small corral to hold his horses, or to brand a few calves in, and so he got busy with the materials he had been given free. Fran took a picture of those old corrals for me. I was no longer able to ride that distance.

Bluff corrals were often used in rimrock country, too. In a narrow canyon near the Hassayampa River on the western edge of the Hozoni the tall bluffs were used as the sides of a corral and across the upper and lower ends of the canyon wire gates, with numerous willow staves, were built. Cattle or horses could be driven down the brushy draw and easily confined there in the natural enclosure.

Many wire corrals were on the Hozoni, too. Some were large and had handy loading chutes, while others were small and would hold only a few cattle—but all were thickly staved with willow limbs and tied with baling wire.

On our way to town we passed the remains of a large, divided rock corral that had once held many cattle or goats. (That brushy country had been used for raising Angora goats, as well as cattle.) After many years, the old rock corral was still standing and in fair condition. On a neighboring ranch a rock corral that was built in 1878 was still being used.

Round horsebreaking corrals made of cedar posts were common in northern Arizona where there was plenty of timber. The posts were set in a solid circle with only a gate interrupting it. Later, discarded railroad ties were used in the same manner. Though one might see the remains of those old corrals while going through the country, you could see new ones as those materials are still being used.

During Bob's early cowboying days rope corrals were much in use, and they are still used on some ranches. A large remuda can easily be controlled with a single circle of rope. There again, the cowboy used what he had on hand. One form of rope corral is where four or five cowboys form a circle around the horses; then, taking their lariat ropes, each man holds onto two ends of rope. After the mounts for the day are selected by the horse roper, the ropes are coiled up and replaced on saddles, and the remuda is free to graze once again.

You might ask, "How does a single rope hold a bunch of horses? Can't they jump over it?" Yes, they could, but they won't because they are trained not to early in their life. Bob explained it to me this way: Along with being halter broke and sacked out, a colt is also taught to respect a rope.

Not only their corrals, but their cabins, too, showed that a rancher starting out on a shoestring was (and is) a right resourceful fellow. I often stopped at the ruins of their cow camps to daydream about those early days, to stand near the little toppled cabins, to walk into the remains of the old corrals, and to take pictures—for those camps would soon all be gone. And always I saluted and admired those old-timers who used the materials Nature gave them to build their corrals and homes, those early builders of our West.

CHAPTER TWENTY

Coopers' Shipping Day

Bob and Charles had helped the Coopers three days with their fall cattle gathering and had found several head of our livestock in their lower Hassayampa River country. Today, we were going to bring them home in our bob-tail truck. I'd been invited to Coopers' shipping day and their noon lunch so I'd taken along a dessert to share.

As we approached the Cooper Ranch, I could hear cattle bawling and cowboys urging the shipping cattle into the board corrals to be weighed. Velma, Nel's daughter-in-law, was at the scales looking lovely in a colorful hat. (I asked permission to take a picture of her for my photo album.) I could smell wood smoke and boiling coffee, and the faint aroma of green chilies bubbling in a pot of pinto beans.

Nel, dressed in blue jeans, red plaid shirt and a western hat, was at her two cookfires tending the beans and removing the coffee pot after adding a dash of cold water to settle the grounds, then she pushed the pot close to the fire to keep it hot for tired cowboys who had been at work since daylight bringing in the cattle from their large holding pasture.

This was a family operation and had been for many years, back when they raised angora goats and hired Mexican cowboys. On this day Nel's sons, Bob, John, and Roy, were riding; also John and Velma's two children, Mary and John Jr. Nel was cooking and Velma would weigh the cattle and keep records.

We parked our cattle truck and got out. I placed my chocolate cake beside the boxes of raised donuts at the end of the long picnic table which was made of several planks situated across two saw horses.

"Good morning!" Nel said. "Coffee?" she inquired. She spoke with a slight Texas accent, I noted.

"I'd love some—didn't get my second cup this morning. Bob was in a fizz to get down here," I laughed.

About this time our mailman pulled up to the row of mail boxes and delivered the mail for the surrounding area. He walked to the table and got a plastic cup before going to the cookfire for his coffee, feeling comfortable to do so. It was evident he'd been to Coopers' shipping day many times before and it made me think of restaurants where regular customers kept a cup and were free to help themselves to coffee.

Mary, a pretty girl in her teens, rode up on her blazed-faced sorrel. They were a handsome pair and I snapped a picture of them, and then I took one of Nel near her cookfires, too.

"We have a new teacher at the Walnut Grove School. It's her first year to teach," Nel said.

"Yes, Joanie told me—I met Ruth, the bus driver, recently, when I went up to get the children with Joanie."

"Did you notice the rock corral on your left as you were coming in? We used to work our angora goats in there when we moved up here to get out of the summer heat near Congress where we wintered. There's a cow trap near the corral, too." When she saw my puzzlement she explained. "A cow trap is a roomy corral with a one-way gate that swings in but not out. Ranchers used to lure cattle out of the rough country into them with water and feed. Few cow traps are used anymore. I don't know why. They were effective."

"So you've always been a ranch wife?" I asked. 'Did you ever get lonely for Texas?" "I subscribed to a newspaper from my hometown. When we went for our mail in Congress there would be several newspapers in the P.O. Box. I'd take them back to camp and sort them out according to dates and read one each day until we went for our mail again, which wasn't very often."

So that was how she'd coped with the isolation and being away from her family and friends in Texas, difficult for such a friendly woman I felt sure.

"Have you ever lived in isolation?" she asked.

"Yes, for eight years on an old packmule outfit in Burro Creek Canyon. I loved it there and so did my son, Mike. We were too busy to get lonely very often."

"What news do you have from Mike and his family?" Nel asked.

"It's dry there. Mike and his friend, David, are irrigating pastures, just as we are here. Realtors are showing the farms on a regular basis. We hope our family can move here by next spring. Sure miss them. It will be good to be together again."

Nel said, "We have a telephone down at the house. Feel free to use it anytime." Then she said, "Get a plate and help yourself to the food. It's mostly beans and coffee. Cowboy favorites."

"Ours too," I said, as I noted the cowboys coming toward the table.

After we'd eaten, the men cut our cattle out of the bunch and drove them up the wooden chute and into our truck. We stopped at the Hozoni mail box and retrieved a big batch of mail, much of it for my folks, and one letter from the publisher who had bought "A Horse of His Own". They wanted more stories. Mom had several letters from pen pals, I noted. This would be her way of coping with isolation. Dad preferred living out of town. He would spend his days reading and tending his spur and gun collections, polishing them faithfully. Someday they would be Mike's. Bob would be busy with ranch work and I would write and submit more articles. And so the pattern for our days had begun.

Chocolate Sheet Cake

Sift together into a large bowl:
  2 cups flour
  1-1/2 cups sugar
  3 tablespoons cocoa
  1 teaspoon soda
  1 teaspoon cinnamon
  1/4 teaspoon salt

Add:
  1 cup cold coffee
  1/2 cup buttermilk
  1/2 cup oil
  1 large egg

Beat, then bake in a greased 12 x 15 inch sheet pan, 15 minutes in a 400-degree oven. Allow to cool a few minutes before punching holes with a toothpick all over.

Icing:
  2 tablespoons margarine
  3 tablespoons cold coffee
  2 tablespoons cocoa
  1-1/4 cups powdered sugar
  1/2 teaspoon vanilla

Combine ingredients in a sauce pan. Bring to a boil. Pour hot icing over cake. Sprinkle 1/4 cup chopped walnuts or coconut on top.

CHAPTER TWENTY-ONE

Christmas Memories — Old and New

Bob and I were sitting by our Franklin stove enjoying its cozy fire one evening three weeks before Christmas when he said, "We aughta go to Prescott and buy more groceries in case we have a hard winter." Putting by for winter was a practice we'd always followed during our Burro Creek days, 72 miles from town, and it was still a prudent one now that we were living 52 miles from Prescott on the Hozoni.

"We need to finish our holiday shopping and mail the kids' gifts—I want to call them, too," I replied.

And so the next morning we drove to town for our Christmas ham and boxes of candy for neighbors and friends, as well as a huge supply of groceries.

On the way home we stopped at our big mailbox and were surprised to find sprigs of beautiful Arizona spruce tied together with a red velvet ribbon, a gift from Nel Cooper. Another surprise was an attractive handmade invitation to the Walnut Grove Christmas program.

Since I attended a one-room country school in Michigan and Bob attended one in Texas, we were pleased our grandson, Todd, would receive his grade schooling in one also.

I remembered the family-type atmosphere we'd had with only nine pupils in the Willis School where my Mom was the teacher. I recalled the whispered plans for May baskets full of flowers and goodies that would be secretly delivered to fellow students and neighbors. Also, the blushes (and delight) when an admirer put a Valentine in the big red Valentine box for the school party.

But of all the joyous memories of that rural school it was the annual Christmas program that stood uppermost in my mind. For weeks ahead the parts and songs were rehearsed at school, while at home bright costumes were made and proudly tried on. At last, the afternoon arrived for the dress rehearsal. That night the entire community would turn out. There would be a large pine tree beautifully decorated and the muslin stage curtains, hanging in place across the front of the school room, would be freshly laundered. And behind that curtain little actors would be nervously going over their lines—right up to curtain time!

We were eager to attend the Walnut Grove program. It was the perfect way to begin the Christmas holiday.

On the appointed night, Fran and Charles followed us to the school in their truck. Mom was riding with us; Dad had decided to stay home to rest and recover from a recent cold. When we approached the schoolhouse, that had served the community since the early 1920s, we noticed luminarias lining the road. It is a southwest custom but one we'd never seen in use. Luminarias, or "farolitos" as they are called in some places, are colorful sights during the holidays. The little lanterns are made by filling brown paper sacks with two or three inches of sand in the bottom to support a candle or votive.

The young school teacher was at the door to greet us. "Welcome, Merry Christmas!" she exclaimed, then turning to Mom she said, "I've heard you are a retired teacher."

Mom's face was glowing when she replied, "Yes. I have a lot of precious memories of those years and I still receive letters from several of my students." Then she said, "This is your first school I'm told. Hope you're enjoying it."

"I have only five students this year, and yes, I am enjoying it."

We went inside and found seats for the five of us. Excited, giggling children were peeking out from behind the curtains to catch a glimpse of the audience. Soon all the chairs were full. The lights dimmed and the program began when a student announced that the theme for their program would be Christmas Cards with each scene to be acted out. The curtains opened and two boys stood singing Christmas carols beside a large, simulated candle and we had the feeling we were indeed seeing an old Dickens' scene of early England. Other scenes portrayed an American Christmas, an English Christmas, a Spanish Christmas, a Medieval Christmas, and the First Christmas, all beautifully acted out in costumes.

While backgrounds were being changed behind closed curtains, the audience was entertained by the students with recited poems and piano solos. Several times we were asked to join in and sing traditional Christmas carols. (Only once was it necessary for the teacher to peek behind the curtains to quiet the excited, noisy preparations for the next scene.)

Then, just as the program ended, we heard a commotion outside, followed by loud pounding on the door. A rancher sitting at the back of the room went to see who it was and there stood Santa Claus!

"Come in, come in!" the rancher invited.

"Ho, ho!" Santa laughed as he looked over the crowd. "I got all your letters. Have you been good boys and girls?"

"How good did we have to be?" one worried child asked. Fran chuckled quietly beside me.

"Pretty good, just pretty good," Santa replied with a smile. Appeased, the child looked at the bag of toys expectantly.

Santa asked a little, blond-haired girl, "Did you help your Mama with the dishes?"

"We have a dishwasher," she promptly announced, drawing hearty chuckles from the crowd and an amused expression on Mom's face.

Santa confided, "I'm going to have a new reindeer next year. Be thinking of a good name and drop me a card."

The teacher's twin girls began planning, "Let's see. . .what would be a good name for the new reindeer?"

Finally, Santa began distributing his gifts from the big bulky pack and expectancy could be felt by everyone. One by one the five grade school children received their gifts and the little pre-schoolers had gifts in the pack, too.

A tiny girl toddled up to Santa when her name was called and smiled a toothy grin at him. The next name called was that of a shy little one who hid her head on her Mama's shoulder, so the baby's big sister delivered the gift to her—and drew a happy smile.

Santa began talking about leaving for other places where people would be expecting him. The little blond-haired girl sidled up close to him and said, "I haven't seen your reindeers yet!"

But since no one ever gets to see Santa's reindeer he hurriedly said, "I have to go now." However, the child followed him to the door for just one glimpse of the faithful helpers waiting there for him. He turned and waved good-bye to all of us, saying "Ho, ho, Merry Christmas!" Then he saw the little girl and paused while her mother whispered a hurried word to her. She turned, and Santa quickly eased through the door. With a jingle of sleigh bells and merry shouts, "Get up there, Donner—we've a long way to go!" St. Nick sped through the clear, cold night.

While refreshments were being served, ranchers talked of rain and fat cattle and good horses. Ranch wives talked about their long lists of things to do before the holidays. Children examined their new toys and sampled goodies from their Christmas stockings. It had all happened many times and in many places before in one-room country schools, only the names were changed in this traditional scene. Still, with it, the magic of Christmas surrounded us, drawing our ranching and mining community close.

Later, the teacher and her five pupils gathered at the door to say good-bye to us all. And still the magic was there; people lingered to experience every last minute. Then, one by one we called our farewells, carolers would come to visit us at the ranch one night soon and we'd have cookies for them near glowing kerosene lights.

As we journeyed home there was little talk. Our minds were filled with thoughts of long- ago Christmases and programs in one-room country schools where happy memories were made and the magic spell of Christmas could be felt.

Mom's Ice Box Cookies

1 cup white sugar
1 cup brown sugar
3 eggs
1 cup lard or Crisco
4 cups flour
1 teaspoon baking powder
1 teaspoon soda
1 teaspoon cinnamon dash of salt

Cream sugars with eggs and shortening. Measure baking powder, soda and cinnamon into flour. Sift into sugar mixture. Mix and form into a long loaf. Wrap in waxed paper and let stand overnight in refrigerator. To use cut into 1/2 inch slices and bake in 350-degree oven.

Mom served these fresh cookies to friends when they dropped by to visit and have coffee. She made good fresh perked coffee. I was allowed to have half a cup for breakfast beginning in the sixth grade.

Ranger Cookies

1/2 cup shortening
1/2 cup white sugar
1/2 cup brown sugar
1 egg
1 teaspoon vanilla
1 cup sifted flour
1/2 teaspoon baking powder
1/2 teaspoon soda
1/2 teaspoon salt

Cream shortening with sugars. Add egg and vanilla. Sift flour, baking powder and soda together and add to batter. Mix well.

Add 1 cup of each: chopped nuts, oatmeal, chopped dates and raisins, and coconut. Mix together with hands. Drop by teaspoon onto greased cookie sheet and bake in 350-degree oven about 15 minutes.

After we moved from the Ozarks back to Arizona Mary Swearengin often included a recipe or two in her newsy letters and I enjoyed making them, assured they would be delicious because she is a talented cook.

Easy Cookies

1 cup chocolate or butterscotch chips
2 tablespoons butter
1/4 cup peanut butter
2 tablespoons sugar

Stir in 1 cup crumbled graham crackers. Spread in greased 8 x 8 inch pan.

Graham-Cracker Brownies

2 eggs, slightly beaten
1 cup graham-cracker crumbs (fourteen 2-inch crackers)
1/3 cup brown sugar
1/2 cup chopped nuts
1/4 cup sugar
1/2 teaspoon vanilla

Mix all ingredients in a large bowl. Spread in greased 8 by 8-inch pan. Bake in 325-degree oven about 20 minutes. Cool slightly before cutting into 2-inch squares.

This is a good make-ahead dessert that freezes well and is good to eat while still frozen, too, as my grandchildren declared when they were my official testers of new recipes. We had lots of fun cooking and testing new foods for my cooking articles in The Western Horseman.

Mom's Corn Casserole

1 15oz. can cream-style corn
1 egg
10 soda crackers, crumbled fine
3/4 cup milk
1 tablespoon minced onion
Salt and pepper
Paprika
Parsley flakes

Place corn, cracker crumbs, milk and onion in greased baking dish. Stir and season with salt and pepper to taste. Sprinkle top with paprika and parsley flakes. Bake until lightly browned, about 1 hour.

Fruit Cake

4 eggs, beaten
1 cup sugar
1 tablespoon cooking oil
1 tablespoon molasses and apple juice
1 teaspoon vanilla
1 teaspoon lemon extract
1 cup flour
2 tablespoons baking powder
1 teaspoon salt
3 cups dates, cut in half
1 cup raisins
1 cup chopped nuts
1/2 cup pineapple chunks, drained
1 lb. fruit cake mix

Combine eggs and sugar, add oil, molasses and apple juice, then vanilla and lemon extract. Sift flour, baking powder and salt into batter. Fold in dates, raisins, nuts and pineapple.

Bake in two greased bread pans about 1 hour in 325-degree oven. A glaze of brown sugar and water may be poured over the loaves, also whisky, if desired.

CHAPTER TWENTY-TWO

Mike Returns Home to Arizona Ranchlife

I spent several days writing, cutting and polishing a story about a horse Bob had been very attached to for several years, and he to Bob. I titled it "Booger, the One-Man Horse", and submitted it to American Horseman, who had bought "A Horse of His Own." I was very pleased when the new story was accepted in just a few days. Now I could turn my attention to writing about Dad's spur collection, and reviewing a book the Prescott Library had obtained for me about spur history. This was big topic for me and would take much time, which I had jolly little of, but I threw myself into the project, collecting information from Dad and the library book. I gave it my all, squeezing it in every spare minute.

I recall Bob saying, "I'll keep the interruptions off you this winter so you can write." It warmed my heart, and I went in my den each morning to write an hour as soon as I'd cooked breakfast and straightened the house. I was determined not to neglect my household duties or my family because of writing. My free hour fell between breakfast and lunch preparations which began at 10:30. A tight squeeze with no time for interruptions.

I finally submitted the spur article. It was refused. The rejection letter stated, "We're swamped with this type of material."

But Collector's World wasn't. They bought it and asked for more articles.

And then it happened! A letter from Mike saying the Missouri farms might have sold. He had been managing them in our absence.

We hurried to the telephone at Kirkland Junction to talk with Mike and learned the prospective buyer had made a deposit on both places. We were to receive cash for our home place and a lease with option to buy on the second place, where Mike and his family lived. It couldn't have happened at a better time now that we were in the middle of another Arizona drought, with the possibility of losing the ranch if it continued. "Droughted out" is the term used when weather has defeated a hard-working rancher. That chilling possibility was something Bob lived with all our married life, and that fear had soon overtaken me as well. But now, by selling the farms we had some financial slack, a relief from low cattle prices and drought expenses which often occur during dry times when ranches reduce their herds and the market is flooded. It's a double whammy.

Fran and Charles were going to Phoenix several times a month now, hauling feed to the ranch in our cattle truck. They were gone on this chore, and Bob was showing our sale cattle out on the range to two cattle buyers when I heard the truckload of cattle we were expecting from Missouri. It couldn't have arrived at a worse time! I was cooking a full lunch for the men. With Bob and Charles both gone it fell to me to accept the cattle, a responsibility I hadn't assumed before but the cattle needed to come off that truck! They were very drawn and some were banged up, but strong, I was relieved to see—and a calf had been born on the trip. He was riding up in the front seat with the truck driver, looking perky and contented.

I returned to the house to complete lunch and boil a pot of coffee to comfort me after my hectic morning.

Immediately after lunch the cattle buyers left, having given Bob a deposit on the livestock they had purchased and would receive at a later date. Bob and I went out to feed the cattle. To ease their stress, we fed them in the same way they'd been fed all winter in Missouri. Bob threw out the hay from the back of the truck, calling, "Come on, Mamas," while I drove in a large circle in the pasture. It was satisfying to see them fill up, poor hungry creatures.

Three days later the second load of cattle arrived with three cows and one calf dead! Tears filled Bob's eyes when he saw what had happened to his "pretty girls." And to make matters worse some of the cows refused to claim their calves and would not allow them to nurse. The babies would have to be bucket fed. Bob's golden palomino saddle horse, Nugget, had ridden with his back against a rod since Amarillo, which could have injured him. It was a heck double heck! Should we sell the remaining 72 cows still in Missouri? Would the other horses and two bulls be killed or crippled? Bob had some very hard decisions to make; we were going to lose money if we sold because the Missouri cattle market was way down.

Finally, Bob decided to have the cattle and two horses (Little Man and Todd's horse, Chuck) shipped to the ranch, taking a chance. The day the truck arrived with them all in good condition was a tremendous relief. Nugget began to whinny at Chuck and Little Man—and they to him—well before they were unloaded, a horse reunion that was heart-warming to hear.

Our kids would arrive in about three weeks, barely time to complete preparations. I wanted to ease the move for Joyce Mae so I decided to help her by painting the ceilings in their house a beige color she had chosen; she would paint the walls with the colors she liked, now purchased and waiting. She'd had a difficult winter with ranch buyers looking at the farm and going through the big ranch-style house that she loved. Leaving would be painful.

Dad was repairing and varnishing a little wooden school desk we'd found upstairs in the stage house. It would be ideal for Todd and I planned to put it in our large kitchen, all ready for him when he came over to visit. There he could sit and color in the books I'd purchased for him and look at his little picture books while I cooked.

On April 22 our family drove in to the ranch with tooting horn and gleeful faces. Mike was pulling a U-Haul trailer. David was close behind with irrigation equipment which we would use around the house and on small pastures down the creek near Logan's Arena. Every bit of ground would be planted in grass.

Bob and Charles came over just as Mike was unloading Todd's tricycle and his collie dog, Lady, putting them inside the fenced yard with Todd who immediately began playing, making motor sounds. I hurried to my kitchen to begin cooking.

Our long anticipated day had finally arrived. The last of our family Caravan West had arrived safely on the Hozoni.

CHAPTER TWENTY-THREE

Old Friends

That last spring and summer was spent battling the drought by hauling alfalfa cubes to the long wooden troughs and irrigating oats in the new lower fields. Mike went to Phoenix for feed often and sometimes Todd went with him.

We had three groups of friends visit us that summer. My high school friend Mary Ann and her husband Bob Berman came to tent camp for three days on their way to Santa Fe. It was terribly hot the whole time. I kept lots of tea and coffee in the refrigerator ready to ice. Flies were pesky near their tent and at the picnic table on the patio. We'd never had such a serious problem before! I was disappointed for them but we did have wonderful visits and recalled the box of dress-up clothes we'd played in. Our long-time friendship was renewed and thrives happily today.

Our Arkansas friends, Charlie and Jerry Horn, had recently moved to Prescott and they came down to the ranch one weekend. I was pleased to entertain them and return the hospitality they had shown us while we had looked for a farm in Arkansas years before.

A few days later we woke to find the Witte Light Plant was on the blink again. Our mechanic was summoned. He would fly his plane to the private airstrip on the Diamond 2 Ranch, 10 miles from the Hozoni.

On the morning he was due to arrive we heard the plane circling headquarters twice to announce his arrival. Everyone went outside to wave at the plane before it turned toward the air strip. Todd was wildly excited and he rode along with Bob to pick up the mechanic.

Meanwhile I got to "rattling my hocks" (got busy in the kitchen) as Bob would say. My journal reminds me I prepared whisky steaks for lunch, hot potato salad, cornbread, tomatoes from our garden, chocolate sheet cake, and iced tea (with mighty few ice cubes.)

The power plant was back in operation later in the day and Todd wanted to ride with us to the airstrip and see the airplane take off. He and I sat in the cockpit while the mechanic loaded his tools, then we climbed out and went back to our truck to watch the plane depart. It taxied down the strip, gathered speed and became safely airborne; we waved good-bye and were answered by the tipping of a wing.

At home, I checked the frozen foods in our big freezer in the garage and was relieved to find nothing was thawing. My main concern had been for our recently butchered beef.

Hot days dragged on. Finally storm clouds gathered and the ranch received six inches of rain! The creek roared past the houses, covered the foot bridge, and deposited debris in the fence separating the pastures. Of course, we were overjoyed with the much needed moisture.

I spent the following three weeks writing a proposal for a food column to The Western Horseman now that my sourdough articles had been accepted with favorable reader responses. I titled the column "Western Flavors" and after Mom and I tested the recipes I mailed it in with mixed expectations. Would they accept the proposal? No. . .but they did like the short stories and recipes and planned to combine them into a longer article. I was pleased they liked the material, and not too disappointed about the column. After all, I was a new-comer to the magazine. (Several years later I did have my weekly food column in the newspaper *The Sun-News* after moving to New Mexico.)

I immediately began work on a second sourdough article which was accepted by the magazine several weeks later.

CHAPTER TWENTY-FOUR

Suzie

One day Bob returned from visiting the ranch south of us with this news, "You'll never guess who I saw down there. . .Old Brownie."

"Our Burro Creek Brownie?" I asked. He was one of the horses we'd sold when we left the ranch six years before.

"Yep," Bob replied.

"Did he remember you?"

"Yep. He nickered at me," Bob said with a pleased expression.

Then I noticed an Australian Shepherd puppy riding in front of him, snugly buttoned inside his jacket. It was the pup Bob had been promised and I suspected another very special cowdog had arrived in my life, and I would be nursemaid to this pup who would eventually go with Bob to work cattle without a backward glance. But, in the meantime I'd heat bowls of milk, clean up little foot prints—and occasionally puddles—and laugh at his cute puppy pranks. I wouldn't have missed having "Pup" for anything!

Through my 31 years of being a ranch wife I'd mothered many cowpups. First Patches, an English Shepherd puppy, had bounded into my life fresh off the train. She was a mail-order bride for Bingo, our talented Australian Shepherd cowdog. We wanted puppies from Bingo so he could train them to work cattle.

Soon Hanna puppy waddled into my life while we were visiting Bob's family in Texas. She was a brindle-colored Catahoula leopard dog, a breed of dog known for tracking hogs and wild cattle in southern states. She rode back to Arizona on my lap.

Later, Pup-Pup (Hanna's coal-black son) and I became best of friends after he howled his way into my life one cold night on the stock farm in the Ozark Mountains. But he too wanted to pursue his life's work and trotted off to work cattle with Bob and his mother, although he was always happy to return to me and the comforts of home where his favorite chair awaited him and juicy meat scraps would be in his bowl. It was easy for me to forgive his brief departures from home and hearth because I knew he loved me and would return panting and happy. By then I understood cowdogs and their need to work, and I loved him enough to allow him that freedom.

Soon after our move to the Hozoni Ranch old Sam fathered a batch of puppies with Boots, a lion hunting dog with white stocking feet. One of her puppies tip-toed into my life. She was a shy little shadow of a puppy with a gray coat and white markings on the tip of her tail and toes. She faithfully followed me for days while I attended my morning and evening chores outside and soon I moved her from the dog pen into the house on her own rug beside my chair and close to the fireplace while Pup had his rug beside Bob. I named her Suzie.

Pup had reservations about Suzie's advancement into the house and hearth and he quickly let me know about it in no uncertain terms. Suzie had been caught sleeping on our bed and shooed off. Directly I found Pup up there with a defiant look on his face, and the following day he brought a bone into the house, leaving it on the carpet in the middle of the dining room floor where I couldn't miss seeing it, a stunt he'd never pulled before. Oh dear! I had a jealousy problem to handle, which I did by giving him more attention and that soon altered the situation which had been both sad and comical.

My quiet, gentle Suzie had chosen me for her companion but I steeled myself for the day when she would leave me to work cattle as the others had done. That day never came. She chose to stay home with me when the cowdog crew left for work, which flattered me out of my boots! And she never changed her mind, but chose to be with me always and allowed no one but me to pet her.

Suzie was very fond of graham crackers. I decided to teach her some tricks using the crackers as rewards. Although she was still quite young she had been easily house broken and I suspected she was highly intelligent as her grandfather Tobe had been and her father, Sam.

I decided to teach her several tricks. She loved it—and the crackers even more. We started it with 'sit' and 'speak', advancing to 'dance', then 'flatten', which she never really liked and it usually required my repeating the command twice before she would lie down and stretch out on the floor. 'Say your prayers' came later—and sometimes she would sneak a peek at me between her paws!

We would go through the routine every morning and she had polished it until her responses were quick, except for 'flatten' which required a cracker reward before the performance.

One day she and I were preparing to go through her routine when Mike came into my kitchen. "I want to show you something," I said as I took the graham cracker box out of the cupboard. Suzie snapped to attention and went through all her tricks willingly even though she had an audience for the first time.

"That's pretty darn good," Mike commented, a little surprised that such a young puppy had learned those tricks. But I was the surprised observer one day when she jumped into the two-wheeled antique cart in the back yard and tilted up and down with a pleased expression on her face. "Teeter totter," I said. We incorporated it into her act, and sometimes she would do it just for my attention without a cracker incentive. A born ham!

So, I was offended when a lion hunter came by the ranch to visit with Bob and he remarked despairingly, "What are you doing with a hound dog in the house?" I was so surprised at his remark that I was speechless. . .hurt. Didn't he have any intelligent dogs in his hunting pack? Surely he did. Or maybe he'd never given them a chance beyond hunting. To him they were just working dogs, which is why he had them, of course, but why had he criticized my care of Suzie?

As time went on more interesting facets of Suzie's personality emerged. Although it is commonly known that some dogs can feel jealousy, I was surprised to learn she was concerned I might be jealous over her and Pup's games. One day I had been petting her sleek coat when Pup edged in for his share of attention. Then he decided to romp with Suzie but she seemed concerned about my feelings because she would romp with him briefly, then come to me. She'd romp with him again and quickly return to me. That was the first and last time I ever witnessed an animal's concern over not causing jealousy. My dear, faithful Suzie; how glad I am she tiptoed into my life.

CHAPTER TWENTY-FIVE

Kitchen Haven

I always liked to think of my ranch kitchen in our rambling old house as being a haven. It was a cozy spot filled with the yeasty aroma of sourdough bubbling in a crock, of spicy applesauce cooking on the range, of freshly boiled coffee steaming in the granite pot to be served with plump sugar cookies or crunchy oatmeal bars or rich chocolate brownies.

My country kitchen was roomy. It had space enough for an inviting rocking chair, a child's old-fashioned school desk, and a large table with eight chairs clustered around. A collection of bottles and jars (found on three country places) sparkled on the shelves in the window, casting blue and green and purple rays on the wall while gingerbread boys danced on the curtains; a room decorated for grandchildren.

Suzie would lie snoozing in the sunshine that streaked across the floor. I'd pat her sleek, gray coat. Dear Suzie. She and I would keep each other company when Bob was gone for the day.

I'd sit at the long dining room table with a mug of steaming coffee and look out the paned-glass windows, enjoying the valley sprawling before me; the historic stage house; the antique farm wagon; the sorrel mare and her colt grazing in the tree-lined pasture. I'd listen for a nickering horse, the jingle of spurs. Meanwhile, steaks would sizzle in a cast-iron skillet and sourdough biscuits would rise and turn golden brown in the oven; the noon meal would be waiting in my country kitchen haven.

CHAPTER TWENTY-SIX

Rain, Rain! Where Are You?

Roundup continued, Mike rode with Bob and Charles. Our cattle truck went for more feed every week and the drought hung on and on. Joyce Mae began her painting project; I cooked and baked for us all. Sometimes Todd came over and sat at the little desk, which he loved, and sometimes he and I went on a short hike with his Lady dog who always stood between us and any perceived danger such as cows, horses, and other dogs. Life was settling into a comfortable routine—if only we could get rain!

Bob contacted a cattle buyer. He bought the steer yearlings and cull cows and left a deposit check for a May first delivery. On the appointed date the cattle were sorted and weighed on our ranch scales. Livestock prices were dismal that spring so Bob retained heifers that he would sell later as grown cows. The ranch expenses had to be cut to the bone. We could not afford so many cowboys. Fran and Charles went to work on a ranch in Oracle, Arizona. Their final check was one of the most painful ones I ever wrote. I received a letter three months later from Fran saying she was pregnant, and later an announcement of Karen's birth. I wished I could have seen her, held the little red-haired baby girl who looked like her father, and eventually had her mother's interest in orphaned animals.

Time marched on and from my June 3, 1972 journal I wrote: "Got up at 2:30 a.m. when the dogs' barking woke us. Bob checked outside but found nothing wrong so he went back to bed but I stayed up to do some work that needs quiet concentration. I heard a coyote's lonely howl and our dogs' answer. Probably that was why their barking had woke us."

From my diary again, "The bank inspector came a few days ago and I prepared lunch while he and Bob toured the range. He's pleasant and puts one at ease and he was very complimentary about Bob's ranch management. He commented on the way we keep up the ranch and said it was a pleasure coming into our house. His report to the bank was vital and our livestock loan could suffer if things weren't up to standard; we'd spent considerable time making it so.

"Bob and I are tired out, having done so much work all spring. We hope to go on a little vacation soon. (But we didn't due to cattle illness—shipping fever that needed medication.) Prescott horse races and summer activities will begin soon. I'm looking forward to visiting old friends on weekends and eating out with them.

"At 5:00 this morning the sky is rosy-red as I look out my studio window. Using the back door, I have stepped outside. The air is fresh and the sounds of early day are around me; the rooster's crow, the morning birds' chatter, a young calf's bawl and its mother's consoling moo. My coffee tastes good. I am refreshed and ready for the day. Will it bring rain?"

We had a surprise birthday party for Bob on June 1, a potluck on the picnic table in the patio. Mom and I made pumpkin pies and Joyce Mae made a potato salad. Later Bob cranked a freezer of ice cream and Todd came over to watch.

A few days later we were making ice cream for David's birthday when dark clouds gathered and it began to pour! Bob and I ran to rescue the puppies and chickens from their flooded pens. David drove down to the creek to get the irrigation pump pulled up to higher ground while Mike drove Mom and Dad's vehicle, his truck, and the tractor farther away from the creek. Just in time! In a matter of minutes rain water poured off the hillsides, roared over the wooden foot-bridge, demolishing it, and swept past the houses.

Bob and I stood on the screened-in porch to watch and smell the pungent aroma of moisture on dry ground.

"Smell, just smell it!" Bob exclaimed. When it was over we went outside to check the rain gauge and discovered over an inch of rain had fallen!

Later, we all sat around the long dining room table sharing David's ice cream and giving excited thanks for the blessed rain. The ranch would need far more rain to end the drought and grow grasses, but this was a start. David's stay with us would soon be over. He'd had the experience of working on an old-time cattle ranch but Missouri beckoned and he was desperately homesick for it, poor man.

The next day Bob and I drove to see how much rain we'd received in the Ward and Robert's areas. "Chasing rain" we'd always called it, and if we were riding horseback Bob would have removed a spur and dug with the rowel to see how far the moisture had penetrated.

On this rain chase we learned only a shower had fallen on the Ward area, but at Robert's Camp the stock tank was nearly full! Of course, we would have liked a heavy rain everywhere, but on a 40-section semi-desert country we were glad for any moisture we'd received. It was early June, leaving time to get more rain and grow fall feed, if we were lucky.

The air was fresh and invigorating and the wildlife was enjoying it. Two perky ground squirrels scurried across the road, jaunty with tails held up. Soon a roadrunner ran past with a snake dangling from his mouth. I hoped it was a rattlesnake.

In this lower elevation I noticed saguaro cacti were in bloom. They appeared to be wearing spring bonnets with their yellow and green trumpet-shaped flowers sitting high on top of majestic arms. When we drove through the wire gate at Robert's Camp brush was in full bloom. It smelled exactly like freshly cut peaches.

On the way home Bob spotted a dogie calf bawling for his mother who was nowhere in sight. Poor little fellow. His stomach was swollen from hunger of long duration. The cowboys had brought in several orphaned calves recently. Their mothers had no milk for them due to the drought and lack of feed. Often the calf was loaded on a horse and brought home riding in front of the cowboy to be fed, then given to one of the milk cows.

"There's a dogie!" Bob pointed to the Hereford calf. "Get him!" he said. I hopped out of the truck and ran toward the baby, who darted away from me. "Get him—get him!" Bob was encouraging me.

I "bawled" at the calf. He stopped to listen and I was able to grab him. We loaded the little fellow in the truck bed. I kept looking back at him and noted he stood up all the way home, appearing to enjoy the ride.

When we arrived at the home corrals I hurried to Todd's house to get him while Bob mixed a pan of warm calf manna (powdered milk) for the hungry little orphan.

"We'll call him Sancho," Bob told Todd. By now the barn animals had come out to say "Hello." Old Sam, several horses and the milk cows, all came to the fence where he was eating, and when he finished with his meal I "bawled" and he followed me and the empty food pan into the alley where two white calves spent their days. Sancho bawled at them, they sniffed noses and wiggled ears, then he bawled across the fence at the other calves. Sancho was home.

CHAPTER TWENTY-SEVEN

Stormed In!

The rains came and came and came the winter of 1972. Phoenix was flooded in places; many other parts of Arizona were isolated for days and we on the Hozoni Ranch were among them. Our mail piled up in our large box, even the four-wheel drive couldn't cross the washes and ravines where angry flood water had tumbled and roared through the mountains and wiped out our footbridge. But I fried lots of chicken to celebrate, as I'd always done in Burro Creek.

Hobbies were pursued and parties were held from house to house. It was wonderful to curl up near the wood fire with a good book and listen to the rain on the roof! Also, I baked a lot during that time and Todd was often with me. One morning we cut out horse-shaped cookies and later frosted them to resemble our remuda, some with blaze faces and stocking feet and even a mule cookie with long ears and nose to resemble Josh, the mule Bob had recently purchased. Todd was enchanted as I finished each one for him to identify since he knew all the horses by name.

Just as we were completing our cookie remuda Mike came in to admire them and said to Todd, "Your Granny and I used to cut out cookies when I was a little boy." "And that's how I knew little boys like to do it," I replied happily.

On and on it rained while we rejoiced over that blessing. I was testing recipes for another sourdough article at the time. Joyce Mae and I were making cookies, cakes, and muffins with our favorite sourdough starters. Ten o'clock and four o'clock became sampling times. Mom would come over and with hot beverages we would critically examine the flavor and texture of the newly developed recipes. Everyone on the ranch took a keen interest in our baking. Dad wanted soft sugar cookies to go with his coffee and I was able to provide him with them; the cowboys just wanted desserts of any kind, and more than once they were seen sniffing the air hopefully. When a cowpoke says, "It shore lays in your flank, Ma'am," you are being paid a high compliment and that recipe is a keeper.

When the flood water subsided, Bob, Mike and Todd started out to estimate the road damage and discovered it was extensive. Only one mile from headquarters, where lower Oak Creek flows through the valley, it would require a caterpillar to repair the road. Fortunately, we'd bought one with the ranch. Mike started it up without any difficulty and began to repair the damage. Bob and Todd followed in the truck. When they reached our mailbox at Wagoner, Todd retrieved the mail, putting it in a brown paper sack for safe keeping. Also there was a note from Nel in the box saying they were okay.

When early spring arrived I began yearning to go camping. But since we were in the middle of a ranch project, I did the next best thing, much to Todd's delight. He and Joyce Mae helped me carry rocks from the creek bed and we built a rustic firepit in the back yard, like one makes upon reaching a new camp. The following day we served camp beans, roast beef and sourdough biscuits baked in the Dutch oven. It was fun and would appease me until I could get to the line camp and cook outside. Spring branding would begin soon, giving me ample days in camp cooking for the cowboys. I lugged out my little chuckbox and cleaned it up all ready to take to our line camp where it would serve as a cupboard and work counter.

Dad's Gold Nuggets

Make a sponge:

    1/2 cup warm milk

    1/2 cup sourdough starter (recipe on page 144)

    1/2 cup pre-sifted flour

Mix and let stand in a warm spot 1-1/2 to 2 hours. Then, cream together and add:

    1 cup sugar

    1/2 cup shortening

    1 egg

    1 teaspoon vanilla

    Beat well then add

    2-1/4 cups pre-sifted flour

    2 teaspoons baking powder

    1/2 teaspoon salt

Knead lightly 4 or 5 times on floured board. Cut out cookies and place on greased sheet to bake in a 400-degree oven 10 to 12 minutes.

Gold Dust Icing

    3/4 cup powdered sugar

    3 tablespoons Tang

    2 tablespoons soft butter

    Enough cream to make stiff icing.

Beat well and spread on Gold Nuggets.

Spring wildflowers came up in glorious profusion and one day Bob rode down to the Golden Aster Mine to check the cattle. When he returned home he presented me with a lovely bouquet of gold poppies and blue lupin. I was surprised and pleased at his thoughtfulness as I had been very sick with the flu for several days.

CHAPTER TWENTY-EIGHT

Cook's Helper

"The school bus couldn't cross the river!" Todd exclaimed as he hurried into the kitchen where I was assembling the roundup foods. "Can I go to the line camp with you today, Granny? I'll help you."

I looked at his eager young face and saw his expression explode into joy when I said, "Yes—you can be cook's helper."

"I'll go tell Mama you said yes!" He exclaimed as he darted away.

Old-time ranch cooks often had a young helper or "button" as they were sometimes called. I surely could use a button this morning! Just about every imaginable thing had gone wrong to detain me, including a fight among the cowdogs. I was thinking about roundups I'd ridden and wondering why the first day is always so intense, when Todd returned wearing his western hat and blue jeans, ready for the day's adventure. "How long have the cowboys been gone?" he asked.

"Ages! They're making a cattle drive into camp," I replied.

The men had loaded the empty chuckbox and bedrolls in the truck before they mounted their horses and rode over the mountain to begin their cow work on the lower half of our ranch.

"Todd, please go open the chuckbox and I'll hand you the groceries," I requested. "I see you baked a lot of cookies!" he said, eyeing the coffee cans I'd filled with chocolate drop cookies. "I'm getting a little hungry."

"As soon as the truck is loaded we'll have a cookie," I promised.

Before long we had the chuckbox stocked and all the other gear loaded. "Think I'll ride back here," Todd commented from his seat high on the mound of bedrolls where he sat eating the promised cookie.

"Let's see how many animals and wildflowers we can count along the way," I suggested. The four-wheel drive truck roared past the bunk house, the white board corrals, the red barns; then wound up the hill. The lovely spring morning was a joyous sight as we drove through the rugged mountains and started winding down toward the line camp.

Due to winter rains and snow, the semi-desert range was covered with green grass. In the distance high mountain peaks were still topped with snow, while far below yellow and purple and pink wildflowers were spilled across the hillsides in beautiful contrast.

The melting snow was the cause of the swollen river that Todd's school bus couldn't cross, but by tomorrow the river would probably be down and he would be at his desk in the one-room country school. He would ride home in the cattle truck with Mike tonight.

Todd shouted, "Cactus blooms!" when he spotted the gorgeous magenta colored blossoms.

"Ground squirrel!" I called, chuckling at the little creature as he scampered away, his bushy tail pointed straight up.

Later I stopped the truck and pointed toward the mountainside where a doe and her fawn stood on the crest of a hill. Like statues, they remained perfectly still silhouetted against the horizon.

We continued on our way and an hour later we saw the windmill and cabin nestled far below in the valley. I listened for cattle bawls and cowboys but heard nothing, then suddenly cowdogs came bounding up the road to greet us and I caught a glimpse of cattle standing in the tree-shaded corral.

"Hi, Grandpa Bob!" Todd called. "I'm cook's helper today—the school bus didn't come!" "I'm glad to see you cooks. Whatcha got handy to eat? I lost my pocket lunch in a brush thicket," Bob said.

"Cookies," Todd volunteered.

"I'll split my sandwich with you," I promised. "We have fruit and milk, too."

We ate in the shade of the huge cottonwood trees and waited for the other cowboys to arrive with their cattle. Soon a breeze came down the valley and the windmill began to pump.

"Quick, Todd, get us some fresh drinking water!" I said. He grabbed the canteen and bucket and darted toward the droning windmill to collect water from the spigot. Meanwhile, Bob chopped wood and built a campfire while I began sweeping the cabin.

"Watch out for rattlers," he warned.

I peeked cautiously under the iron cots and into corners, then checked the wood cookstove for packrats' nests. Thank goodness, they hadn't built one in the oven this year! How had they managed to squeeze in before?

Todd arrived with the water just as we heard cattle running down the mountain trail. Bob quickly mounted his horse and rode out to give the cowboys a hand, while Todd and I hurried inside the cabin to be out of sight until the herd was corralled.

"Hold up there. . . easy, mamas. . . easy!" a cowboy shouted.

"There comes Dad," Todd whispered as we gingerly peeked out the window. Mike was in the lead of the herd trying to settle them down. I watched as he soothed the leaders, talking to them, riding with ease in his saddle. Cowdogs barked and finally surrounded the cattle until they had no way to escape. Suddenly the ruckus was all over.

When the cattle were corralled I put the coffeepot on the cookfire to boil water and set out the cups, ready for tired cowboys. Todd had gone to the corral to ask, "Did you see the wild bull, Dad?" He'd heard about the bull that couldn't be gathered; was so mean he chased cowboys and horses when they tried! But plans had been made to rope the bull and tie him to a tree to settle him down before anyone attempted to drive him again.

"Not today, Son. I see you're Granny's helper," Mike commented as they walked toward the cabin. "And I see you made a sun dial."

We'd learned the shadow would travel one inch an hour in the eight-inch circle with a stick in the middle. Todd had checked it several times while we waited.

While the men drank their coffee my little helper carried armloads of firewood into the cabin to replenish the woodbox and I began settling. Before long our camp was in order and he went to the corral to watch the men work. And soon he was fetching water for thirsty cowboys and lugging firewood to their branding fire.

Later, when our cattle truck was loaded with livestock ready to be hauled up to headquarters Todd hurried down to the cabin to tell me goodbye.

"You were good help," I said. "See you Saturday."

Early Saturday morning he would return to help me again. This time he'd bring his bedroll and sleep under the stars, and just maybe the notorious bull would be in the bunch when the cowboys rode in with the cattle. At any rate, the "button" would have the experience of being cook's helper like children on long-ago cattle ranches before him.

Chocolate Drop Cookies

1 cup brown sugar
1/2 cup butter
1/2 cup buttermilk
1 egg
1-1/2 cups flour
1/4 teaspoon soda
1/4 teaspoon baking powder
4 tablespoons cocoa

Cream brown sugar and butter together. Add buttermilk and egg. Combine soda, baking powder and cocoa with flour, add to buttermilk and egg. Drop by tablespoons onto greased baking sheet. Bake 20 minutes in 375-degree oven.

These cookies can be iced with a powdered sugar and cocoa frosting but I usually left them plain when they were to be stored in a large coffee can and taken to the line camp.

CHAPTER TWENTY-NINE

Reliable Help

Mom, Todd and I were selecting books in the bookmobile at Wagoner when we saw our tan ranch truck approaching.

When it arrived Mike said, "Bob's had an accident. Get in, Mama. I'm taking him to the hospital."

Bob's face was ashen. He was slumped forward in the seat, stunned. Mike gave me only the briefest account. This was no time to discuss it in front of Bob, to recount the horror of a favorite horse bucking and kicking him while he was helplessly hung up underneath.

Pulling water-gap fences after a creek rises was a spring and fall job in Burro Creek Canyon, and now on the Hozoni. The barbed wire fence spanning the stream would be lying on the ground, allowing cattle to pass through. We had always used a horse and rope to pull the fence tight, after clearing it of debris. On this particular day Bob and Mike were working on the water-gap fence west of our house. They'd cleared the barbed wire when something spooked Steamboat and the frightened horse began to buck. He made several pitches. "I thought Bob was going to ride him. I couldn't see any light at all. He was really screwed down in the saddle," Mike later recalled.

But suddenly the frightened horse began to spin, wrapping the rope around Bob three times. Immediately the saddle turned to the side! Steamboat began kicking at it—and Bob! Mike ran to free him. His head was hitting rocks and sand in the creek bed. Mike grabbed the bridle and backed the horse, which immediately stopped bucking. When Mike helped Bob to crawl out from under the horse, with broken ribs and beaten hand, that he'd put up to protect himself from Steamboat's kicks, his first concern wasn't his injuries. It was his pistol! "It's got sand in it!" he shouted angrily.

We started toward Prescott, leaving Mom and Todd with Nel and Roy Cooper. Nel called ahead to our doctor's office but when we arrived at the hospital we learned he was on vacation so another doctor would be on the case. He ordered X-rays of Bob's ribs but not his hand nor his head. Why more X-rays weren't taken I'll never know. Due to our shock we may not have described the accident fully.

And so there we were in the hospital with a new doctor rather than our old friend caring for Bob. Mike drove back to Cooper's Ranch to pick up Mom and Todd and to ask Joyce Mae to pack a suitcase for me. To make matters worse we were worried about Joyce because she had suddenly developed a lump on her throat and Mike was to take her to Phoenix to see a specialist in a few days.

The day Mike and his family were in Phoenix, Mom and Dad fed the chickens and dogs and Dad turned the dogie calves in with the milk cows and then grained the horses outside in the long wooden feed trough. My folks could always be counted on to help on such occasions, in spite of Dad's failing health.

We learned that Bob had multiple rib fractures and bruises all over his body, possibly a concussion. It was painful and serious; he would not be riding the roundup.

Four days later my cowboy was ready to go home. The rough ride into the ranch wasn't as hard on Bob as I had feared it might be. The Hozoni looked mighty good to us!

Pup met us, wild with joy, and stayed by Bob's side constantly indoors and out. It was then we learned Pup had refused to eat for several days while Bob was in the hospital. Joyce had fixed enticing food for him, which he finally accepted half-heartedly. Poor Pup, if only he had known his friend was recovering and eventually they would work cattle together again, but he had smelled the blood on Bob's clothes and was afraid.

Mom and Dad greeted us with smiles and words of cheer. Bob immediately went to his favorite chair to rest, with Pup on his rug beside him.

I noticed Joyce Mae had vacuumed our carpets and cleaned old food out of the refrigerator, even though she was feeling no better. We were very frightened for her, and waiting for the medical report would take several days.

We would need a cowboy to help Mike with the fall work. Word was out at the Palace Bar and feed stores that the Hozoni needed a cowboy. Fran and Charles were sorely missed but they had moved back to Missouri by this time.

When Bob went for his checkup, his doctor was pleased with his progress. We went over to Joyce Mae's doctor's office to see if they had heard anything about the Phoenix report, and were relieved to learn that the lump was a benign cyst that wouldn't require surgery! We hurried home with this good news. Thank God, the frightening medical prediction hadn't come true.

Things were turning around. Now, if we could just find a cowboy.

CHAPTER THIRTY

"Creek"
The Friendly Ghost

One morning a cowboy arrived at the ranch. He'd been sent up by the Wickenburg saddle shop. Bob interviewed him and learned he'd cowboyed in South America and was eager to get back to working cattle. Our rough terrain didn't concern him, so Bob hired Kevan for the roundup and he drove up to the bunkhouse to settle in.

The ranch received eight inches of rain that October, a record. Mike and Kevan rode whenever weather permitted and several neighbors came to help them from time to time. (Five weeks after his accident Bob was back in the saddle working cattle on Steamboat.)

Joyce Mae and I began hiking every morning with Todd and his Lady dog. The doctor had prescribed exercise and vitamins to improve Joyce's health. The hike soon became a welcome activity. Sometimes we went a mile to an abandoned two-room cabin where a gold miner and his family had lived in the 1930s. Grapevines were hanging from the trees and Todd loved swinging on them. Occasionally, we took our lunches with us and sometimes we walked farther west where another miner had lived. He had built a rock fireplace in his cabin and a rope swing with an old-fashioned board seat was still swung from a tree, indicating a family had lived there. This place was very appealing with its many things to explore and the rope swing for Todd to play on.

Near Halloween, Todd and I carved a jack-o-lantern in one of our garden pumpkins and that day he put on the bear costume his mother had made for him and he went to trick or treat at every house, wearing the paper sack mask he and I had made. I'd prepared him that Burro and Creek, the friendly ghosts, might come to visit him if he kept the porch light off.

Later that evening Mom dressed in her long Centennial costume she'd made while in Prescott, and I draped a white sheet over my clothes. We knocked at the door, and I said in a deep voice, "Wooo! I'm Creek, a friendly ghost!" when Todd opened the door. He paled but responded admirably. "Come in," he managed to reply in a quavering voice.

"Nooo. We just came by to say hello and happy Halloween." He gave a weak smile then offered to share his candy with us. His smile broadened when he saw our popcorn and fudge gifts. "We brought you and your family some goodies to munch on," I said, letting my voice become more natural.

When I drifted away in my white sheet and pink house shoes he looked down at them and exclaimed, "Granny!" I think deep inside he'd know it was me all the time because we were always playing games: wagon train adventures, cooking imaginary meals, stabling our stick horses in a small wire corral, riding those frisky horses across the hillsides. Yes, deep inside he'd probably known it was me.

One Halloween years before in California I'd made a monkey costume for my six-year- old son, Mike, to wear to his school carnival and I dressed up too. When I went in the Ladies Rest Room wearing a mustache and my organ-grinder costume the women shrieked. I hadn't said "boo" and I sauntered out to reclaim my little companion waiting outside in his monkey costume with tail draped over his arm.

It's a toss-up who had the most fun, the monkey or the organ-grinder; the friendly ghost or the three-year old.

CHAPTER THIRTY-ONE

Seasons For All Things

We awoke to the persistent jangle of the alarm and hopped out of bed to begin the holiday preparations. Bob built a crackling fire in the little Franklin stove, then went out to feed the dogs while I stuffed the Thanksgiving turkey. Afterwards, I took a cup of coffee to the studio and sat contentedly looking out the window. The first pink glow of sunrise streaked across the sky, silhouetting Silver Mountain. The horses trailed in for their grain; two cowdogs bounded past the window, romping and playing. I heard a calf call for its mother and her answering bawl and the lonely wail of a coyote on a distant hill. Lights clicked on at the bunkhouse and soon wood smoke curled up from the chimney. Farther up the draw the choreman's light had been on since 4:00 a.m.—it always was. And then I heard baby Tara crying next door, eager for her morning bottle.

This Thanksgiving morning, I was more thankful than ever that everyone was well in our valley, since a series of accidents and illnesses had befallen us in past months. Stealthily, insidiously, they had entered each home and touched each person in our family. This continued off and on for months, wave after wave of it. Meanwhile, a severe drought hit us again and the cattle market dropped out of sight. Then a crushing blow came when my beloved Dad passed away. Finally, a ray of sunshine shown through our clouds the morning Joyce Mae came to tell me she was expecting a baby in October. It had been an exciting fall for us all while we awaited the baby's arrival. Joyce Mae was in good health so preparations for the new little one were enjoyed. There had been some discussion about Joyce Mae staying in town the last two weeks of her pregnancy, but thinking she would have plenty of warning, as she had with Todd, the idea was discarded. But, frankly, I was jittery; I studied a book about emergency childbirth and baked a sheet and towels in a low oven to sterilize them as the book instructed. We almost needed them all: on October 29, at 6:00 p.m. Mike drove her and me up to the hospital emergency entrance—and one hour later our precious Tara was born. The next day I bought a little pink dress for her, the first baby girl in our family.

Still thinking about that happy, hectic day, I went to the kitchen to prepare breakfast and was basting the turkey when Mike came to show me the round piggin' string he had braided.

"Happy Thanksgiving!" we exchanged greetings. Then he told me he and our hired hand were planning to rob a bee tree later in the week. Thoughts of hot biscuits and fresh honey were mouth-watering.

Mid-morning, Todd arrived to see the browning turkey and inquire about the potluck menu. We decided to list the foods on colorful paper and post it on the door: turkey and sage dressing, mashed potatoes and gravy, candied yams, green beans, cabbage slaw, fruit salad, cranberries, rolls, and for dessert, pumpkin and mince pies.

Mom came over to set the table and help me. We chose a dark green linen table cloth and arranged a fall decoration of leaves, wild gourds and Indian corn spilling from a straw cornucopia. Light green napkins and brown pottery dishes completed our table setting.

At noon everyone on the ranch began to arrive with their foods. Bob carved the turkey, with Todd looking on with interest. "Can I have a drumstick?" he asked hopefully. (Children always want a drumstick, don't they?) That reminded me of a

Thanksgiving dinner in Burro Creek when we'd invited Mom and Dad and a young couple and their two children from the Yolo Ranch. We'd served turkey and all the trimmings that year also, and the little three-year- old had enjoyed the turkey so much that he kept requesting "more chicken." It had been a happy holiday filled with festive foods and good guitar music, provided by our friends. Good happy memories stored from our isolated ranch so long ago.

After dinner on the Hozoni, we gathered in the living room to plan Christmas and soon decided it should be an old-fashioned holiday with traditional foods, a flickering fire in the Franklin stove, glowing kerosene lamps, and a tree trimmed with handmade decorations. We would make fudge and crackerjacks and homemade cookies, and have them ready for the Walnut Grove school children when they came to carol everyone on the ranch.

Baby Tara fell asleep on the divan. Mike went to reload shells and later to practice shooting. Meanwhile, Todd and I played a game of Old Maid, while some of the others played rummy. The afternoon melted away happily, then one by one our guests went home. The family would return for a supper of leftovers, served on paper plates this time. Mike would deliver a plate of food up to the bunkhouse.

Later that night, lights clicked on at the houses and wood smoke curled up from chimneys. Bob and I sat before our fire, entirely too full, but contented, for it truly had been a day of Thanksgiving.

CHAPTER THIRTY-TWO

'A' is for Apple

Old-timers told us the five apple trees on our ranch were planted by a homesteader and his family. In later years the trees were sometimes neglected due to their isolated location. But like persistent pioneers, two tall gnarled trees had endured. Their roots had sought out the water from the little creek that trickled past, some distance away. And when everything suited their needs during the spring and summer the trees gave us their juicy red prizes in the fall.

But once we were disappointed to find all the apples had been picked when we arrived at the old orchard, bundled up against the fall chill and anticipating recipes using the tart red apples. Someone had beat us there and the trees were bare!

Thereafter, Mike saddled up his horse and packmule and went a week early to fill several gunny sacks with the luscious fruit, leaving a few for the unknown person who had enjoyed the jewels in the past

We hung the sacks on nails in the old stage stop where they would stay cool, though I'd learned the fruit didn't keep long and I'd hurry to make applesauce, apple butter, and apple pies like my grandmother taught me to make in 1945. I always thought about her every time I made apple pie. (Still do.) I think about her twinkling blue eyes and her tiny 90-pound figure with a neat, fresh apron tied around her trim waist.

And when I went to the store room for apples I thought about the old-timer. . .was he surprised a few apples had been left on the tree for him?

Sometimes apple dumplings, basted with a thick brown sugar syrup, awaited my husband when he came in from the evening chores, which always brought a happy smile to his face, because this recipe was from his childhood.

Mother White's Apple Dumplings

    6 tart apples, peeled and cored
    6 tablespoons sugar
    1 teaspoon cinnamon
    6 tablespoons butter
    pie crust enough for 2 crusts

Roll out pie crust and cut in circles. Cut apples in half. Combine sugar, cinnamon and butter. Place apples on crust. Spoon sugar, cinnamon and butter in center.

Place in baking pan and bake 10 minutes in 425 degree oven, then 30 minutes more in 350 degree oven.

Baste with the following syrup:
    2 cups brown sugar
    1/2 cup white sugar
    1/2 cup water.

Boil a few minutes before pouring over dumplings. Baste several times during the baking period.

CHAPTER THIRTY-THREE

Another Christmas

"Twas the night before Christmas. . .," I began reading aloud the poem Clement C. Moore wrote for his children in 1822. My grandchildren snuggled close to me, enjoying each word of the beloved old poem. It was Christmas Eve. Our tree was trimmed, gifts were wrapped, baking was done. Tomorrow would be a big day.

When Todd and Tara had scampered home next door, my husband Bob and I sat before the Franklin stove reminiscing. "Remember the year we had the old-fashioned Christmas?" I asked. "That was fun!" Bob nodded and puffed on his pipe as we recalled that holiday, and the day it was planned.

Everyone on the Hozoni ranch had gathered in our house for Thanksgiving dinner, and afterwards we'd congregated in the living room to visit and make Christmas plans.

"What foods shall we fix?" someone asked, but it seemed we were really too full of turkey to spark much enthusiasm for menu suggestions.

"Shall we draw names?" another offered.

Bob chuckled and remarked, "Might have to give IOU slips again if we get snowed in." "Like we did that time in Burro Creek!" I exclaimed.

"IOU slips?" Todd questioned.

"We gave them instead of gifts because we got snowed in on our canyon ranch and couldn't get to town," Mike explained to his son. "We wrote on pieces of paper things like, 'IOU a batch of fudge.'"

"Mmmmm," Todd said.

"And Bob took his packmule and hauled our groceries and Christmas presents home the time our truck got stuck during a snow storm," Mike recalled. "I got a train that ran on flashlight batteries that year—we didn't have electricity in the canyon," he told Todd.

Then everyone became quiet and pensive in our living room and seemed to be remembering Christmases past. Suddenly Mom said, "Let's have an old-fashioned Christmas."

"Yes!" everyone agreed in unison. A spark was ignited. The storehouses of memories opened up and ideas began tumbling out. Immediately—and all at once—we were planning foods, gifts, and decoration ideas taken from long ago. "I'll hunt a tree. . .let's make tree ornaments. . .and fudge and popcorn balls. . .I'll steam the suet pudding."

"I hope it snows," Todd said wistfully.

In the days to follow, more and more ideas for our holiday grew, and we hoarded gifts and surprises like squirrels storing their winter nuts. I smiled with satisfaction the day I hid the coconut cake in a safe place to age, since a tall cake, covered with thick white icing and lots of shredded coconut, is one of Bob's childhood memories of Texas.

The days passed swiftly. It seemed I had only blinked an eye and it was Christmas week. As usual we attended the play at the one-room country school in Walnut Grove, 17 miles from our ranch, where all eight grades were taught. After the program we learned that the children would come to carol us the following evening.

So the next day we put the finishing touches on our old-fashioned setting and completed the treats that would be offered the carolers. At dusk we heard a truck motor. Immediately the cowdogs began to bark, and Bob called, "The carolers are here, Ma!"

I lit the kerosene lamps and clicked off the electric lights. A cheery fire crackled and snapped in the Franklin stove. Goodies were hurriedly set out on the table, ready for hungry young appetites. Meanwhile, Bob and Todd had gone out on the front porch, and I soon joined them there as the school children began singing 'Jingle Bells.' When they finished, Bob called to them, "Come in, come in and warm up!"

Amid the ohs and ahs over the decorations, cold little hands were warmed near the fire. Shadows danced cross the walls from the kerosene lamps, and the Christmas tree looked happy. Cut from Hozoni land, it had been trimmed with strings of popcorn, bright paper chains, and handmade ornaments. It reigned over the festivities and seemed to protect the walnut baby cradle that was holding brightly wrapped gifts. Dad had made that cradle for Todd, and it later held baby Tara, too.

Todd proudly invited the children to help themselves to the goodies he and I made: fudge, divinity, and popcorn balls. And there were assorted fancy cookies from the other homes on the ranch.

Later, the children trailed out to the bunkhouse and barn, where the evening chores were being finished. In the star-filled night they began the first strains of 'Away in a Manger.' How appropriate that carol was in a setting where horses and cows were eating peacefully. I thought about the true meaning of Christmas.

When Christmas Eve arrived, Todd's wish came true. Snow fell off and on for hours, covering the roofs, mounding up around the wagon wheels, settling on the branches of bare trees. It was a wet, clinging snow—just right for making snowballs, and sure enough, at chore time I heard Todd and Mike laughing and playing in the snow.

Later in the evening the family gathered at Mom and Dad's home to partake of the traditional steamed pudding. Mom made it the week before Christmas so the molasses and spices would mingle throughout. Why it is called a pudding I don't know, actually it is a type of cake brought to this country from England. The recipe is below.

Christmas morning the age-old greeting rang through our ranch house. Soon I heard the thump, thump of boots being knocked free of snow as the family arrived for the gift exchange.

Joyce Mae had on a long dress for the occasion, and looked like a lovely old-fashioned picture. Before long bright papers and ribbons were scattered everywhere. New gloves were tried on, perfume was sniffed, toys were held. The aroma of coffee and browning turkey continued to drift into the living room until Bob asked in desperation, "When do we eat?" I slipped off and returned with the coconut cake and set it beside the mincemeat pies on the hutch. The turkey was carved while Todd looked on expectantly. The menu included such old favorites as cole slaw and escalloped potatoes. Plates were heaped up and conversation was abandoned while everyone enjoyed the food.

The day ended too quickly, it seemed; suddenly the house was quiet. Bob was in his favorite chair, puffing on his pipe; I had on my comfortable robe and slippers. We sat before the fire, quiet and content, for it had been a day to remember. Then I chuckled and thought:

'Tis the night of Christmas and all through the house
Not a creature can stir—not even that mouse!
The stockings were dumped by the fireplace in haste
And thoughts of more turkey is not good to the taste.
Bob in his slippers and I in my wrap
Have slumped in our chairs—completely sapped!
Little Todd is snuggled deep down in his bed
Chubby cheeks are all rosy from play on the sled.

Old Santa is resting, the elves are asleep
Poor Donner and Blitzen—those snowbanks were deep!
But our walls echo back the sounds that we heard
From loud little squeals to the soft loving word.
Tired though we are, the memories are dear—
We'll soon rally 'round to shout, "Happy New Year!"

Steamed Pudding

Combine:
    1/2 cup sugar
    2 large eggs
    1 cup buttermilk
    1 cup molasses
    1 cup ground beef suet

Sift together and add:
    2-1/2 cups sifted flour
    1 teaspoon each soda, salt and cinnamon
    1/2 teaspoon ginger
    1/4 teaspoon cloves
    1/4 teaspoon nutmeg

Stir well, then add 1 cup of raisins. Pour into a greased tin mold or tube pan. Set on rack in a steamer kettle that holds at least 3 quarts of water. Cover tightly and steam 3 hours.

Remove pudding from steamer and place in 325-degree oven 3 or 4 minutes to dry top. Store in a cool place.

To serve, place the pudding back in the steamer and steam 10-15 minutes. Cut into wedges and cover with the following sauce:

Sauce

    1-1/2 cups sugar
    2 tablespoons flour dash of salt

Add:
    1 pint boiling water
    2 tablespoons vinegar
    1 tablespoon butter

Cook over low heat until clear, about 5 minutes. This recipe will serve eight to ten people. If you have any pudding left over, it can be reheated and served another day; it will improve with each steaming.

CHAPTER THIRTY-FOUR

Modern Sourdough Bakin's

In the old days, in mining camps and cow camps, sourdough recipes were mostly confined to biscuits and flapjacks, with an occasional Dutch oven cobbler or cake. Possibly this was due to a lack of some ingredients commonly used today.

Modern cooks have learned that sourdough adapts itself very well to many other breads and desserts, including cookies, coffee cake and upside-down cake, muffins, and refrigerator rolls. These bakin's keep fresh longer than ordinary baked goods do, and many may be frozen, reheated, and still retain their moisture.

You will need a fresh, active starter—thick and bubbly, and eager to work! Remember, a good starter foams up, bubbles wildly, and then settles down to gurgle happily. We suggest the following starter for these recipes.

Sourdough Starter

In a large bowl or crock, place:
> 2 cups warm potato water (saved from boiled peeled potatoes)
> 2 tablespoons sugar
> 1/2 teaspoon salt
> 1 package dry yeast
> 2 cups pre-sifted flour or 1-3/4 cups un-sifted flour

Mix well, cover, and set in a warm spot to work 12 to 24 hours before using in the recipes to follow.

Finding the ideal place to put your starter is sometimes a problem. It needs steady heat in a draft free location. If you have a gas stove, you can set the starter crock in the oven. The pilot light gives the right amount of heat to activate the yeast. In other locations, such as a cupboard, bowl of hot water beside the starter is helpful; also, some cooks like to place the crock in a bowl of warm water. You will soon learn the best method for your kitchen.

Grubstake Cookies

These chocolate drop cookies keep the cookie jar rattling! Make a sponge of:
 1/2 cup warm water
 1/2 cup white sugar
 1/2 cup sourdough starter
 1/2 cup pre-sifted flour.
Set in warm spot about 2 hours.

Add:
 1 beaten egg
 1/2 cup shortening

Sift together and add to batter:
 2 cups pre-sifted flour
 1 cup brown sugar
 5 tablespoons cocoa
 1 teaspoon baking powder
 1/2 teaspoon soda
 1/2 teaspoon salt

Mix well. Spoon cookies onto greased sheet and bake 10 minutes in a 400-degree oven. They are good plain or iced. Nuts may be added to the batter, too. Here's an icing you might try:

Coffee Icing

> 2-1/2 cups powdered sugar
> 2 tablespoons cocoa
> 1/2 cup strong coffee
> 2 tablespoons soft butter
> 1 teaspoon vanilla

Hozoni Coffee Cake

Make a sponge of the following:
> 1 beaten egg
> 1-2/3 cup warm milk
> 1/3 cup sourdough starter
> 2 tablespoons melted shortening

Let stand 20 minutes in a warm place.

Sift together and add to the sponge:
> 1/2 cup sugar
> 1 cup pre-sifted flour
> 1/2 teaspoon salt
> 1 teaspoon baking powder

Pour batter into a round, greased cake pan and set in warm spot for 20 minutes. Just before baking, sprinkle with this topping:

1/2 cup brown sugar
1/2 teaspoon cinnamon
1 tablespoon flour
2 tablespoons soft butter
1/4 cup ground pecans

Mix well and put on cake. Bake 20 to 30 minutes in 375-degree oven.

Peach Upside-Down Cake

Prepare the Hozoni Coffee Cake batter. While the sponge is resting during the 20-minute period, prepare a butter and sugar mixture in a 10-inch skillet or baking pan:
Melt 3 or 4 tablespoons butter.
Sprinkle 1/2 cup brown sugar over butter.
Arrange canned peach or pineapple slices on butter-sugar coating.
Add nuts or coconut, if desired.

Pour batter over fruit. Bake in 375-degree oven for about 30 minutes. Immediately turn upside- down onto a plate, leaving pan on top for a few minutes so the sugar mixture will run down over the cake.

During the winter of 1972-73 we went to town only five times, but no one was restless. Hobbies were pursued and parties were held from house to house. It was wonderful to curl up near the fire with a good book and listen to the rain on the roof, as Arizona had been burdened with one drought after another.
For days at a time our mail piled up in the Hozoni Ranch mailbox, eight miles from headquarters; then someone would drive out in the four-wheel drive truck through muddy roads and

swollen creeks to "fetch" news of friends from the outside world. On and on it rained. More recipes were tried, among them Oatmeal Muffins.

Oatmeal Muffins

Make a sponge of:
    1 cup rolled oats (quick or old-fashioned)
    3/4 cup warm milk
    1/2 cup sourdough starter
Set in warm place one hour, then add:
    1 egg
    1/4 cup melted shortening
    1/2 cup brown sugar
Sift together and add to batter:
    1 cup pre-sifted flour
    1 teaspoon baking powder
    1/4 teaspoon soda
    1/2 teaspoon salt
Fold in 1/2 cup of raisins, if desired. Pour batter into greased muffin cups. Bake 20 to 30 minutes in 400-degree oven.

Wouldn't they be nice for Sunday brunch? Perhaps served with bacon, or little sausages, and scrambled eggs—plus lots of coffee and peach jelly to spread on those hot muffins.

If you go camping, here is one way to prepare your sourdough starter to travel:

Take one cup sourdough starter. Add one cup flour and form dough into a ball. Place in a sack of flour. When you reach camp, put the starter in a bowl or crock, add one cup warm water and one tablespoon sugar. Beat well and set in a warm spot to work. It may be used in about three hours.

A friend, whose father was a good, old-time camp cook, says, "The sourdough crock was the last thing he loaded on the packmule, and it was the first thing he took off when he reached camp."

Gold Pan Biscuits

Here is a biscuit recipe that is handy, as it can be mixed up and the biscuits put in the Dutch oven to rise an hour or so while you go pan for gold. Actually, many a golden brown biscuit has been baked in an old gold pan!

Combine:
>1 cup sourdough starter
>1/3 cup warm milk
>1 tablespoon melted shortening

Sift together and add:
>1-1/4 cups pre-sifted flour
>2 tablespoons sugar
>1/2 teaspoon salt
>1/4 teaspoon soda
>1 teaspoon baking powder

Mix lightly. Turn onto floured board and knead well. Cut, or pinch off biscuits. Arrange in greased Dutch oven, turning each one over in the grease to coat the top. Cover with a cloth and allow to rise. Bake with coals under the Dutch oven and on top of the lid. Or, in a biscuit pan, bake in 400-degree oven 20 to 25 minutes.

Whole Wheat Biscuits

These biscuits can be prepared in camp, too. They are great with honey!

Sift together:
    1-1/4 cups whole wheat flour
    1 teaspoons baking powder
    3 tablespoons sugar
    1/2 teaspoon salt

Add:
    1 cup sourdough starter
    1/3 cup warm milk

Mix lightly. Turn onto floured board and knead well. Pinch off biscuits. Arrange in greased pan, turning biscuits over in the grease to coat the top. Set in warm place and allow to rise 25 to 30 minutes. Bake in 400-degree oven 20 to 25 minutes.

A good hand with a Dutch oven can bake many breads, cakes and cobblers in camp. Beginners, go easy on the coals—it takes far fewer coals than you'd imagine!
Meanwhile, back at the ranch. . .

Cook's Help

This refrigerator dough is prepared ahead, all ready for a busy day when work time is short but appetites are big! Make a sponge of these ingredients:
    1/2 cup warm mashed potatoes
    1 cup warm potato water

1 cup scalded milk
1/4 cup sugar
1 cup sourdough starter
2 cups pre-sifted flour

Be sure the starter is very lively—or add 1/2 package of yeast to the sponge (in addition to the starter) to give it a boost. Cover and set in a warm spot three hours.

Then add:
1/2 cup melted shortening
Sift together and add:
4 cups pre-sifted flour
1/2 teaspoon soda
1 teaspoon baking powder
1 teaspoon salt

Combine. Turn onto floured board to knead lightly. Put in large greased bowl, turning dough to coat top. Cover and set in refrigerator. Dough will stay active four or five days.

When hot rolls are desired, remove the amount of dough needed from refrigerator, knead lightly, and make into rolls. Set in warm spot to rise, an hour or so. Bake in 400-degree oven about 25 minutes. This receipt makes four dozen rolls.

Would you like to develop your own sourdough recipes? It's lot of fun! Take a regular recipe and note the basic ingredients, add some sourdough and increase the liquid somewhat. Use a bit more flour, and a bit less leavening—just mess with that old recipe, adding and subtracting, baking and testing until you have the desired results. And that's the way new recipes are born. Sometimes you'll hit it the first time, seldom will you have a total flop. So try baking with sourdough!

PHOTO ALBUM

Mule colt Hank and mare Missy.

This beautiful mule colt is the offspring of a male Ass or Jack and a female horse or mare.

Hank the mule colt explores his new world.

Mike and his '56 Chevy.

David holding Todd, Joyce Mae and Mike in front of the main ranch house.

Mike and Todd during their visit to the Hozoni.

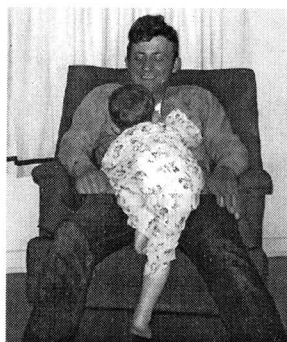

Mike and Todd at the Line
Camp in Burro Creek Canyon.

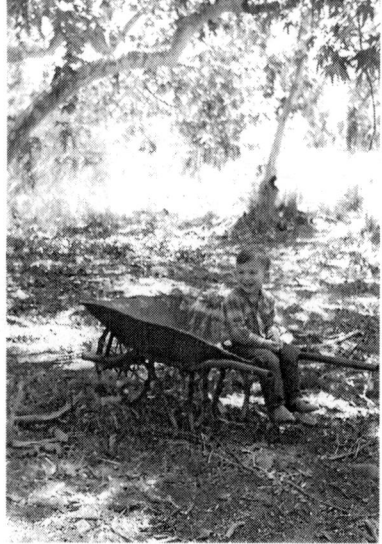

Return to Burro Creek
Canyon. Todd in wheelbarrow.

Joyce White and the old cart where Suzie played Teeter Totter.

Joyce holding Hanna and Todd.

Suzie and Precious in the living Room.

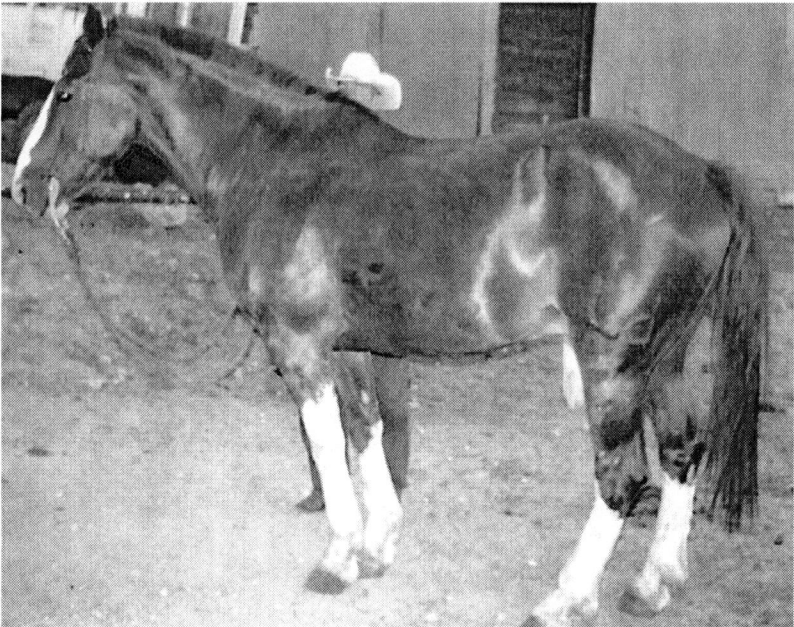

Bob's horse, Steamboat, that almost killed him at the Water Gate.

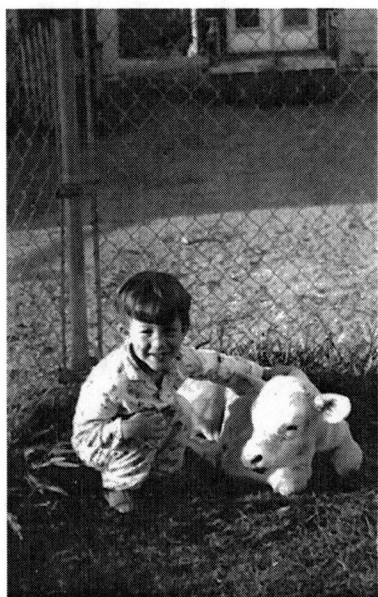
Todd and the calf "Sancho"

Todd in his chaps.

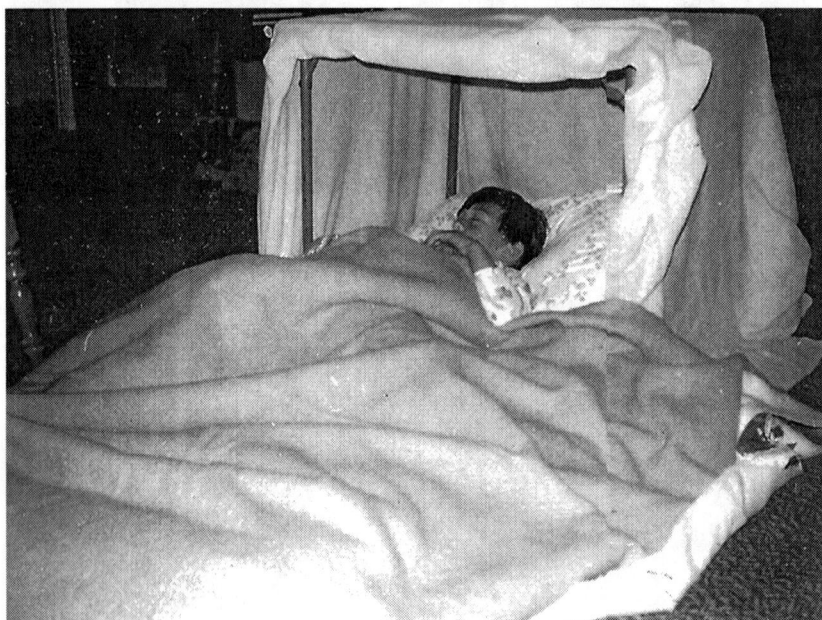
Todd in his tent.

Todd riding Chuck and Bob riding Smokie.

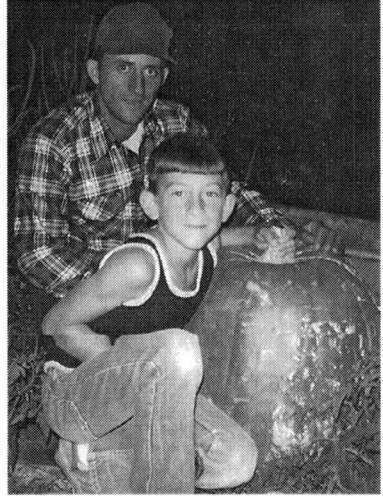

Mike, Todd and the pumpkin.

Thanksgiving on the Hozoni, 1972.

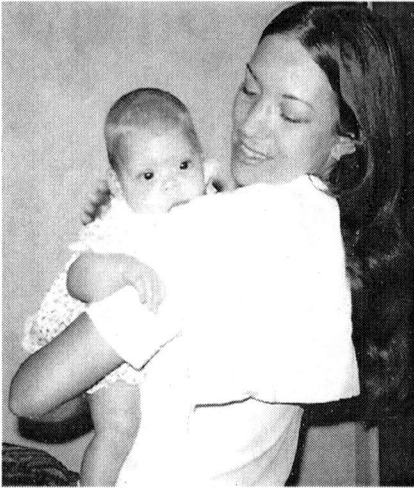
Joyce Mae and Tara

Grandmother Margrey and her great granddaughter Tara White at Christmas time, 1976 (Tara is 1 year old on October 28, 1976).

Tara and Snip.

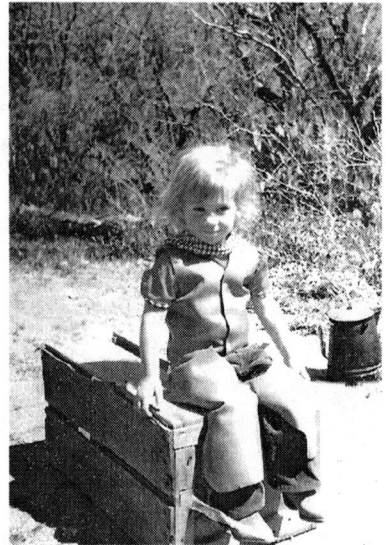
Tara at Robert's Line Camp.

Joyce Mae and Tara in her dining area.

Todd watches as Tara and Snip grow up.

Sourdough Bakin's.

Hearth cooking.

CHAPTER THIRTY-FIVE

Roger

Without looking at my kitchen clock, I always knew it was 4:00 a.m. if Roger's light was on in his camper. As soon as it was light enough outside he would walk over to the barn to fill the horses' morrals with grain, and measure grain in an old coffee can and pour it into the milk cow's feed bucket. Clipboard in hand, he methodically checked off his list of barn chores as they were completed. Doing those chores morning and night freed Bob and Mike to pursue other ranch work. His help was greatly appreciated.

Roger was a small bespectacled man with a ready smile. He had joined us on the ranch when he needed employment after his night watchman's job was completed at a local gold mine. Bob pulled his little trailer to a spot in back of our blacksmith shop where lights and water could be hooked up for him.

Once a month I grocery shopped for him at Safeway, following his short list. Kippers were among the foods he wanted, but we usually tucked treats in the brown paper sacks also.

The morning following our shopping day he would collect his groceries from the back porch. Milk and eggs were stored for him in the refrigerator on the porch, which he was free to access as needed. When we butchered, packages of beef were placed in the freezer for him; garden produce was there for his picking all summer. On my baking days, pie, cake or cookies, as well as buns, awaited our faithful chore man.

Roger soon became an extended family member and was included in our holidays and special occasions. He would arrive neatly dressed in his Sunday suit, eager to share a light- hearted antidote he had heard on his radio, never controversial subjects. He was the perfect guest.

Dad often stopped by to visit with Roger on his morning walks that he took to keep his arthritis pain under control as best he could. Occasionally little Todd went with him also. Sometimes Mom and Dad invited Roger to Sunday dinner, when again he would be dressed in his suit and would have interesting tidbits for discussion from his radio.

He was with us two and a half years until his health began to fail, and he needed to live closer to town and his doctor. Bob drove him to Prescott to apply for social security, and soon thereafter Mike pulled his camper to the KOA camp ground.

We missed the little fellow who had been a part of our family. His choreman duties were sorely missed, too. "He was the best choreman I ever knew," Bob commented later.

Several weeks later Mike learned that Roger had developed diabetes, and that was why he hadn't felt well. For years he could be seen bicycling around town with his basket of groceries. I wish he could have stayed with us; we missed him and the morning light up at his camper.

CHAPTER THIRTY-SIX
The Old Stage Station

Questions about the stage stop kept nudging me and by early spring I'd begun researching it in library books and old newspapers stored at Sharlot Hall Museum in Prescott, an hour at a time while Bob loaded horse feed and visited there at the store. This type of research was new to me, but I enjoyed going through the papers reading bits of news and ads for local stores. And because research is rather like a treasure hunt, I found all kinds of interesting surprises along the way, and ended up studying several stage lines to boot.

The Territory of Arizona had a stage line serving it twice-monthly as early as 1857. It ran from San Diego to San Antonio and was usually called the Jackass Mail since the wagons and coaches were drawn mostly by mules. One of the main stations on that line was Maricopa Wells. Though at first it had been only a small wattle and mud shelter, soon a fine adobe building was built for the Butterfield Overland Mail.

Maricopa Wells was described by Emerson Oliver Stratton in Pioneering in Arizona as: "A rambling adobe structure, one room in width, ran around three sides of a great hollow square enclosing about two acres; in the middle was a huge stack of wild hay. A high adobe wall completed the fourth side. In the center of the wall were large wooden gates for teams, and a small door in one of the gates for people. All the rooms, except the office and the store, opened only into the square. The office, the store, the saloon, and the living quarters faced the road.

One side of the building contained the stables and blacksmith shop. Running down the opposite side was the hotel—meals a dollar per."

Stratton said that the standard meal at a stage station—whether breakfast, dinner or supper—consisted of black coffee, red beans, bacon and biscuits. But Maricopa Wells had a herder who kept 50 head of cattle to supply fresh meat to the hotel in winter and dried beef in the summer. Occasionally a sack of onions or potatoes arrived from San Diego, so Maricopa Wells was more fortunate than most stations.

Across the northern part of Arizona Territory, the Central Mail Co. had established a stage line in 1865, but so many drivers were killed that it had to be discontinued. By 1871, however, there were two steady lines going west from Prescott; one ran south through Wickenburg and on to Ehrenburg, the other line came from the east and ran northwest to Hardyville on the Colorado River.

Business was so good on the Hardyville route that a new road ranch, as stations were sometimes called, was built in 1876 about 12 miles north of Prescott. The American Ranch was a two-story building made of molded adobe bricks. A balcony ran all around the second story. Supported by ornate pillars, it gave the building a colonial look. Outstanding meals were served there to teamsters and stage passengers. The menu included ham, mutton, beef, chicken, fresh eggs, homemade bread and butter, cheese, jellies and jams, as well as dried apple pies. That certainly wasn't the standard meal for stations of that time.

Both the northern and the southern routes had guards to escort the stages through hazardous Indian sections. On one such assignment between Tucson and La Mesilla it was reported that seven guards were well armed with Colts and Sharps rifles.

Soon stage lines began to connect northern and southern Arizona. An 1886 ad announced in the Weekly Arizona Miner that mail was being carried by Wells, Fargo and Co. between Prescott and Maricopa, and from Prescott to Phoenix via Wickenburg. Still, none of these routes crossed our ranch, and my treasure hunt continued for mention of Wagoner or our stage station.

Then I uncovered an old map showing that a horse trail had existed from Prescott to Walnut Grove in 1863, and later that trail extended all the way to Wickenburg, carrying the U.S. mail. Now, I was getting close.

At last I found the first mention of the Castle Creek Stage Co. Although the description was brief, it did trace the route as going through our part of the country, and further reading established that it did stop at our station! The year was 1890.

It seems, however, that the line had been short-lived due to poor roads in the Castle Creek area, and by 1891 it was running only as far as Walnut Grove. The following year the roads were improved and a new billing appeared in the Weekly Arizona Miner. The stage was running regularly, and our little station was busy again in 1892, providing fresh teams for the rough descent onto the desert floor.

The headline on that 1892 billing read: "Prescott to Phoenix, via New Castle Creek Route." The copy read: "Go take a bath— go to Phoenix via the New Castle Creek route and take a bath at the Hot Springs. Stages will run to Phoenix via Copper Basin, Walnut Grove Dam, and Hot Springs from now on. Leave Prescott for Phoenix every Monday, Wednesday and Friday at 8 a.m.; arrive every Tuesday, Thursday and Saturday at 5 p.m. Fare—Hot Springs, $8.00; to Phoenix, $12.00. Excellent stations on that route, where meals are served to travelers at 50¢. Wagoner & Balz Props. James E. Bones, Agent, Prescott."

Let's 'ride' that stage from Prescott to Hot Springs! At 8:00 a.m. one spring morning we pay our $8.00 fare and climb aboard the southbound stage. About three miles out of Prescott we go through Gold Gulch (Forbing Park) and soon we start the steep, winding descent down Iron Springs Road, stopping at Atkinson's Station. Then we pass through brush-covered mountains for many miles before we level off and arrive at Skull Valley for a change of horses. Now the road is relatively level and we can see for many miles as we thunder toward Kirkland, where we will have lunch. We are told that tasty meals have been served here to teamsters and stage passengers since 1864.

Thirty minutes later we are traveling due south and we are in rough terrain. The road winds through the mountains, finally coming to the Hassayampa River. There nestled in a grove of cottonwood trees, is Craig, which has a store, a post office, and a little school nearby. Ahead lay Walnut Grove and Wagoner, where we will spend the night.

Nowadays one would never suspect that the sleeping town of Wagoner was once a busy place, and in fact had been considered as a possible site for the capital. In 1892 it had a two- story hotel, a blacksmith shop, corrals, post office, and general store. In the early 1940s the hotel burned to the ground. The corrals and blacksmith shop were gone. All that remained was the empty general store, dozing with its colorful memories of bygone days.

I learned through oral history and letters to old-timers that supper at the hotel at Wagoner might have included chili, served with cornbread; pinto beans, highly seasoned with onions and chili peppers; venison or beef potpie; and for dessert, either dried apple pie, molasses pie, or mashed potato chocolate cake.

The meal would have cost us 50¢, twice the price as in Prescott where meals were 25¢ at the Nickel Plate Restaurant. Old-timers told me that chili was a very popular main dish. The easily prepared recipe would be ready for cooking in five minutes, and when done it could stand for hours without the flavor being impaired.

During his batchin' days, Bob often fixed chili and set it on the back of the wood range to simmer while he tended his ranch work.

Bob's Chili

1 pound ground beef
1 large onion, chopped fine
1 teaspoon chili powder salt and pepper to taste.

Put the meat, onion and seasonings in a heavy stewing pot. Cover the ingredients with cold water and allow to simmer about two hours. Leftover pinto beans may be added or a can of stewed tomatoes during the last of the cooking. It is delicious served with crisp crackers or cornbread.

Another old-time favorite was vinegar pie—sounds awful, but actually it is very toothsome, and a dandy substitute for lemon pie should you be out of lemons. Along toward spring, when a person hankers for something tart, vinegar pie will surely fill the bill! There are several ways to prepare this pie. Though many recipes do not call for pecans, we liked the nutty flavor they gave to the tart filling. Here is our version of that very old recipe.

Vinegar Pie

Prepare your favorite recipe for pie crust and bake the shell two or three minutes in a 425-degree oven. For the filling, mix together:

3/4 cup sugar
1/4 cup flour
1/2 teaspoon salt
1 teaspoon cinnamon

1/4 teaspoon cloves
1/4 teaspoon allspice
Add:
1-1/2 cups hot water
3 tablespoons vinegar
2 tablespoons butter
3 eggs, beaten
1/2 cup ground pecans

Cook over low heat until slightly thickened. Pour filling into baked shell and bake about 30 minutes in a 350-degree oven.

The following morning we get off to a good start on the second half of our 'ride' to Hot Springs (now called Castle Hot Springs). Ahead of us lie eight miles of steep, mountainous travel. An extra team of mules has been hitched in the lead to help pull the stage all the way to Boulder Pass. Some colorful names for the grades ahead include 'Bull Whacker's Hill' and 'Whoop-e-Up,' which indicate just how rough a ride it will be.

We are glad to reach Boulder Pass and have a 10-minute rest at Goodwin Station (the stop here on our ranch) while fresh horses and mules are being hitched up. Soon the stage winds its way down the other side of the mountain. At the mining camp of Briggs, a bar and a post office are open; and there in this semi-desert country we begin to see wildflowers—blue lupins and yellow poppies. And we smell the peachy fragrance of brush in bloom.

Now we are on the desert floor where a brilliant carpet of purple, yellow, pink and white flowers spread a welcoming mat across the TP Ranch, where Toll House is located. At last, the stage thunders into Hot Springs, making a dramatic entrance. There we will rest, perhaps take mineral baths, and partake of their outstanding cuisine. (Had we taken a fall journey, we could have had roast ostrich for Thanksgiving dinner.)

A few years later, tourists began arriving at Hot Springs via Morristown (east of Wickenburg) on the Santa Fe Railroad, where they were met at the depot by the stage to complete their journey into the desert. An 1898 pamphlet, Resorts on the Santa Fe, describes the 24-mile trip which involved three changes of horses, this way: "Stages run daily. Four hours over a fine wagon road which extends 24 miles eastward from Hot Springs Junction. It is comfortable and quickly reached."

Shortly the transportation from Morristown to Hot Springs was powered by engine instead of horses, though it continued to be called 'the stage.'

Our stage stop on the Hozoni Ranch had played its role in an exciting era, providing fresh horses and mules for the stage that carried passengers and mail. Still in good repair, the Goodwin Relay Station reigned over the other ranch buildings and was given due respect by all persons who examined it.

CHAPTER THIRTY-SEVEN

Adjectives for a Mule

In the 1940s there was a popular song about mules. It mentioned them as being stubborn and stupid with funny long ears and weak brains. For a long time, if we'd had to limit our adjectives to describe Josh, our favorite mule, it would have been comical. Other appropriate descriptions would have been loveable, dependable, and talented, and a baby sitter, too. That mule was a character, and he was a ham also.

Soon after we bought the Hozoni Ranch, Bob began searching for a young mule. My husband had always been a mule admirer, having learned long ago how well they would carry a rider in rough country, which our new range most certainly was.

After several mule hunting trips we found Josh in Wickenburg, where a young couple had a business of buying and selling horses and mules. The woman had taken a fancy to Josh and proceeded to green-break him.

When Bob walked out to their corral and spotted the big dun mule, it was love at first sight. So we bought him on the spot and hauled him home. We soon learned he had no mulish tendencies commonly credited to mules by non-mule lovers such as kicking, biting, or stubbornness, all of which are often brought on by poor handling. Mules are prideful creatures and few will tolerate being mistreated. Since Josh was used to a woman I was talked into riding him in the corral with Bob holding the lead rope. Eventually I taught Josh to back up and overdid the praise, apparently, because he always backed up with a smug look on his face when he desired my attention, saddled or unsaddled. What a character: a ham, a comic, and as lovable as they come.

Bob would often rush to the house to share a new antic with me, saying, "Good gosh, that Josh. . . "

He associated with horses and loved our grandson's young horse that he was very protective of. But Josh clearly knew he was a mule and always buddied up with another mule when possible. Once we boarded a packmule for a friend and Josh quickly accepted his companionship, they were seen grazing together daily.

I recall one day I was hoeing in the garden when Josh and his mule friend came to the fence to observe me. I was wearing a pink sunbonnet and Josh didn't seem to know me until I spoke his name. Then he cocked his ears forward. I went in the kitchen to get cookies for both mules. Josh was crazy about my oatmeal cookies, the same recipe that had won old Bingo's heart in Burro Creek when he was so jealous because Bob had brought me home on our honeymoon.

We'd had our Josh nine years when Bob returned home from branding calves in the lower country one day. He came to the house with this report: "Now I've really got something to tell you—the funniest thing I ever saw!" And I knew I was to hear another anecdote about our long-eared friend.

Bob had roped some calves off Josh and rode back to the truck where he unsaddled the mule, leaving him free to go home for his grain at the barn. Then Bob drove back to the line camp where he put out salt and checked the windmill. All in all it had taken nearly two hours, Bob estimated. Imagine his surprise when he returned to find Josh standing where he had left him! Unsaddled, free to go home—and it was well past feeding time by then, yet there he had waited for Bob. If the saddle had been there on the ground one might think that was why he'd stayed (much like a cowdog will wait beside his master's saddle for long periods of time). But that was not the case and I had to agree with Bob it was the darndest thing I ever heard.

"Let's go home, Josh," Bob had called and his mule fell in behind the truck. When he reached the corral, Josh hee-hawed. Immediately Bob went to the feedroom to get his grain, though he postponed his own lunch to do so.

That morning there was a new word description for our Josh: faithful.

But no one is perfect. The day came when Josh briefly fell out of favor. Bob stomped in the house saying, "That old fool ran away with me! Straight toward our neighbors' mares. That old fool is mare crazy!"

CHAPTER THIRTY-EIGHT

Tin Can Treasures

It was during a clean-up job on the Hozoni that the tin can bug bit me! What had started out as just a big, tiring job suddenly developed into a big, new hobby.

Near one of our line camps, tin cans had been strewn everywhere, so one day while my husband rode to check on the cattle, I began picking up cans and putting them in gunny sacks to be hauled away to the dump. Since mining had been done throughout this part of the country for many years, some of the litter showed to be that of a miner—for example, the walking shoe with its home-repaired sole, and the tiny burro shoe. But when my eyes fell upon the rusty sardine can, which quite evidently had been opened with a pocket knife—that's when the fever began and the tin can bug hit hard! I could almost see my bewhiskered miner as he laboriously opened that can. Then a flood of questions filled my mind about that era, and the search for answers (which makes collecting so enjoyable) followed.

By the time Bob rode back to camp, I had the steaks and Dutch oven biscuits cooking over the campfire. I jubilantly told him about my finds. Having gotten to the bottom of one heap of trash, I considered myself well-rewarded. . .there lay a 1929 license plate. Perhaps the camp is much older, but that plate pretty well established the general date of cans found in that pile.

I began reading books about mining and discovered that some of the mines in this region, such as the Octave, Weaver, and Stanton, were operating in the 1860s. Of course, as is usually the case, the more I read the more questions demanded to be answered. How long has food been canned in tin cans? What sizes were used? Well, it is evident that the tin canning industry has come a long way since it began in England in 1810. The containers were called "tin canisters", and the smallest one used in 1818 was a one-pound, six-ounce size. Here in the United States, when Thomas Kennett and Ezra Daggett received a patent from President James Monroe to improve "the art of preserving" food, the President referred to the cans as "vessels of tin". By 1839, tin cans had come into widespread use in our country. But, then it took a 10-hour work day to make 60 cans. Now manufacturers produce thousands each day!

Further research followed, for by now I was completely overtaken with my new hobby. I'd spot a dump while touring the ranch and I'd yell, "Stop the jeep, Bob! I see a dump!" My husband would put on the brakes and give me a patronizing glance. Once he kiddingly remarked, "We've been hauling off cans for years—now I'll be danged if we aren't hauling 'em back again!" But I'd dart over rocks and around cactus to inspect the pile of rusting cans I'd spotted. (You know how the fever is.) And I'd shriek, "Look here! Look at this! Say, here's a find!"

Collecting fever is catching—soon he was lugging home cans! In fact, it wasn't long before everyone on the ranch was bitten by the bug. Mom went to the library with me for research; Dad went to other mining camps to hunt for more treasures. The cowpokes rode in, smiling and proud, with such prizes as snuff cans.

And soon Mike and his family were calling "Hey, is this an old can, or isn't it?" I didn't know, but I decided to find out—if I could. Letters were sent to several companies and their enthusiastic responses to my questions poured in. Every time we drove for our mail—eight miles from ranch headquarters—more facts had arrived about our hobby. Mail time became a bigger event than ever.

The first reply was from Clabber Girl Baking Powder, telling that their product had been manufactured and distributed as far back as 1899. And, I thought about those golden brown biscuits my miner had baked. Had he used a gold pan for his biscuit pan, and baked them in a reflector oven, as an old mining friend of ours often does?

With his sardines and beans he often ate crackers, too. In one camp, I found an attractive old Premium Crackers container; so I wrote the company for information, and learned that since the early 1920s they'd been using tin cans for their crackers. Due to the cost involved, the tins are used less frequently these days, and are now used primarily for export.

On further expeditions to our deserted mining camps we found many coffee canisters—Folgers, MJB, and Maxwell House, as well as Velvet and Prince Albert tobacco containers, lard buckets, shortening cans, Log Cabin Syrup tins, and evaporated milk cans—just to name a few. By the end of the afternoon, we'd drag home exhausted, sunburned, and exuberant with a gunny sack full of cans, as well as other mining relics.

Many empty Crisco cans were found in the mining dumps; and for good reason, as it has been manufactured since the summer of 1911. A coupon introducing Crisco stated the price as 15 cents a pound, and the earliest can had an eight-page circular cookbook cut to fit the lid. It is interesting to note that the company was the first to give nationwide cooking lessons to American women interested in learning how to cook with the new all-vegetable shortening. Those attending the cooking schools were given free foods and a one-and-a-half pound can of Crisco. In addition, if Crisco couldn't be found in the local grocery, the company would mail the housewife a full-size package for 25 cents. While searching for your "Tin Can Treasures", you might find a very old Crisco can almost anywhere—it even went to the South Pole with Admiral Byrd!

Due to the handiness of canned milk, and the need for it in many recipes, one finds lots of old evaporated milk cans in cowcamps and mining dumps. Carnation canned their first milk on September 6, 1899. The original cans held 16 ounces, and the retail price was 10 cents a can. A very old label (prior to 1903) called the product "sterilized cream". In 1906, the Federal Food and Drug Administration was formed and established a standard of identity for the milk under the current name, "evaporated milk".

We were fortunate to find two Log Cabin Syrup cans. Their blend of syrup was put in those cute little cabins (in honor of Abe Lincoln) from 1887 to the 1940s. During World War II, a reproduction of an antique bottle was made for the syrup. At this time, the company has no plans to use the tin containers again, so hang onto your cabin if you have one.

It wasn't long before I realized we were finding many empty tins that had been used for other purposes after being emptied. As well as storing matches, horseshoe nails, foods, etc., some containers were converted to be used in other ways. Large syrup cans had been given wooden handles, and were used to haul water. The bottoms of coffee and bean cans had been punched full of small holes and served at sieves or sifters—and one can had been cut in half lengthwise, pounded full of rough holes and then mounted on a wooden handle. Cheese or spices were probably grated on this. (In addition, discarded round tops resourcefully covered mouse holes in cabins, too!)

"Now that you've got 'em, what are you going to do with 'em?" What do you do with the old tin cans you have so happily hauled in? First, of course, you sort them, saving only the best, or the unusual. Some are just cans; others have an interesting shape and these you will probably want to keep. Then, order should be given the collection by grouping, and perhaps by labeling with name cards. Also, you will need a colorful background, such as

176

checked oil cloth or old wallpaper. Both are reminiscent of the era.

Since we had already decided to turn the historical old stage station on the ranch into a Western museum, we thought this the ideal place for our new collection. In one corner, on a weathered table, we put a red and white checked tablecloth and arranged a place setting with the food cans in the background. Now they were a real conversation piece (as if a collector ever needed one!).

Upon seeing our collection of tin cans, one guest remarked, "You are doing much the same as an archaeologist when you collect and reconstruct a scene from a camp." He's right. After a while, a pattern forms. It may vary somewhat from camp to camp due to individual tastes, but it could pretty much be reconstructed like this:

The old miner hikes back to camp, weary and hungry—but elated, for he has found color in the creek bed today! He ties his burro to the picket post and begins chopping mesquite for his campfire. In the top of the flour sack, he mixes his biscuits, puts them in his gold pan, and pops them into his reflector oven to bake. Meanwhile, coffee has brewed in the granite coffee pot.

He pours himself a tin cup full and samples it. Contentment is written on his sun-weathered face. He opens the beans with his pocket knife, as the rabbit frying in the Dutch oven sizzles and browns. His dog nudges him—just to remind him that he likes biscuits and 'lasses too! Later, the campfire burns low, the old-timer reaches for his snuff, or tobacco can, and he idly reminds himself to repair his shoe before he starts out in the morning. The burro brays, a coyote calls and is answered in a mocking tone by the dog. . . daydreaming? Of course! But that's part of the fever of the collector. Generally, the more you daydream and reconstruct (with the aid of reliable research), the more you'll enjoy your hobby.

CHAPTER THIRTY-NINE

Company

One day I drove the eight miles to Wagoner for our mail. Among the letters was one from Jeanie, my Michigan childhood friend. She and her husband Olen were planning a trip west and hoped to visit us. It had been 1969 since I had seen her while my family had visited Michigan and we attended a recital of Jean's piano students. It had been a wonderful renewal of our childhood friendship. And now I was to see her again!

We planned to meet in Prescott for lunch, then they would follow us back to the ranch for the night. Bob wanted to give them a tour of our place close to headquarters, and also drive them to the spot where one could see the mountains in far-off Mexico on a clear day.

Only one thing had been wrong. The lack of enough time to reminisce at length about Jeanie's and my farm days; about Two-Bits the collie dog I had given her when our family moved to California to help my aging grandparents; about the free movies her mother drove us to during the Great Depression; the "productions" Jeanie and I gave for our mothers up on the hay loft with Two-Bits as one of the main characters in our plays; about the fancy Valentine box filled with popcorn and homemade fudge her mother had fixed for us, pretending it was from admirers; about the homemade bread and freshly churned butter she had waiting for us when we came in from play.

I can almost taste it now. . .Mrs. Beagle made her bread from a starter stored in her "yeast can", as she called it.

In California, my first friend was Maryann Switzer, who I met at church. Our mothers became friends there also and soon our families were visiting back and forth during the frightening war years, clinging together the day war was declared after Pearl Harbor.

Maryann is of Irish and English heritage. Her tall graceful figure and long legs danced to Mexican music and her clicking castanets, which I greatly admired. When she and her husband came to see us on the ranch, we recalled happy moments of dressing up from the box of clothes stored for our playtime. Sometimes her younger brother pretended with us, but usually not, being a boy dressing up didn't appeal to Buddy.

We were going through a hot drought time on the ranch. I kept tea and coffee ready to ice and we visited about those early days at length, renewing our memories and renewing our friendship, which is strong today, as is Jeanie's. A depression and war had bonded us together. Out of bad had come much good.

Mrs. Beagle's Yeast Can

1. Dissolve two yeast cakes in 1/2 cup warm water and let stand.
2. Boil three medium-sized peeled potatoes until tender in water to cover. Do not drain off the water. While hot, mash the potatoes very fine.
3. Add 1/2 cup sugar and one tablespoon salt. Cool until lukewarm.
4. Add the dissolved yeast to the potatoes and set aside to rise. At this point you can make a 'yeast can' by taking out one pint of the ingredients and placing it in a quart jar. Store the jar in a cool place to be used next time in place of yeast cakes. It must be at room temperature before use.

The yeast can be used over and over by taking some out and adding some new dough back.

5. To make bread, allow the balance of the batter to rise then add enough flour to make a stiff dough. Stir real good at this point. Let rise, then mix in more flour. Let rise again in a warm place. After it has risen for the second time, knead, pinch off loaves, shape and place in greased bread pans to rise until ready to bake.

Note: As in many old-time recipes, no baking time or temperature was given. She baked her delicious bread in her woodstove oven until brown on top. Years later whenever I baked yeast bread I always thought of dear Mrs. Beagle and I came to realize her 'yeast can' was a type of sourdough starter. Wonderful bread, wonderful memories of a comforting time in the Great Depression.

CHAPTER FORTY

Rattlesnake

It's a miracle no one was ever snake struck those 17 years on the Hozoni. Todd's pet rabbit was killed by one while innocently confined in a wire cage in the back yard. Mike's alert eyes discovered one coiled under his truck. Young rattlesnakes, recently birthed, yet poisonous, were found on Mom's back porch, and in Joyce's flower bed. Miraculously no one had been struck!

One morning I started toward the cool stage stop. "Watch out for rattlers," Bob had said before driving off in the jeep. I was recalling his warning as I walked behind the building. Suddenly I heard the buzz of a huge diamondback rattlesnake stretched out on the wooden step, sunning. He began to slither down beside the building, acting as though he had taken that route before. I couldn't allow him access to the uncemented rock wall where he could enter the building and be free to lie on a shelf where an unsuspecting person might be struck.

I ran around the building and grabbed a gardening hoe leaning against the house. I saw the last half of the snake and was able to pin his tail to a rock just above his rattle.

Joyce Mae's front door was open. "Help!" I yelled to her. "I've got a rattler pinned by his tail!" She ran up to our garden and grabbed a second hoe. About then the snake doubled back to investigate what was confining him. He was very angry! Joyce tried to hit him but was unable to do so as he was withdrawing his upper body into the rock wall.

About that time the wonderful smell of browning muffins drifted to us from her kitchen. "Geefie, turn off my oven," she called to Mom whose front door was also open that balmy spring day. "We're busy killing a rattlesnake!" It took a while for her to strike it in a vital spot, while I kept the tail pinned, but she did and we breathed a sigh of relief when it was dispatched. We'd had a 'tiger by the tail', all right. To relieve the tension we all had muffins and hot coffee at Joyce's.

And then one morning Tara and I were in the garden harvesting vegetables for lunch when her sharp young eyes spotted a snake. "There's a gopher snake, Gran," she said. Rattlers and gopher snakes look very much alike but when I saw its broad head I knew what it was. "Get back, Tara! It's a rattlesnake!" I yelled and grabbed a hoe to end the danger. Only minutes before I'd picked a zucchini inches from that snake!

Our cowboy's wife heard the commotion and she walked down from the bunkhouse with her pistol. "Oh, I've been seeing that snake," she remarked. His body had been partly hidden among the greenery. He'd been there to eat packrats who dined on the vegetables. He was so tame that he never rattled!

I still shudder at our close calls, and I had several nightmares the following days. It was, indeed, a miracle that no one was ever snake struck.

CHAPTER FORTY-ONE

Gorgeous George

It was spring and Bob had decided to buy a purebred Brahman bull to be used on the Hereford-Charolais heifers Royal Ranger had sired. They were beauties! A three-way cross would put disease resistance in the herd and we'd get top prices at auction for steers and bulls, as they were much sought after in Arizona. And so Bob inquired about Brahman bulls and soon was directed to Wickenburg where a young woman had one for sale. His name was George, steel gray in color, a handsome fellow who had been gently raised. He could be petted without any problem and he loved having his ears scratched, too.

George was soon living on our ranch with Ranger's cream-colored daughters, now ranging in the Logan arena area. "A fair piece," Bob had said—but not far enough away, as it turned out. As it was spring, Ranger decided to stroll up to visit George's females, a decision he soon regretted. He made his presence known by bellowing. George bellowed back. It was not a friendly welcome. And soon all heck broke loose! Heads were butting and their bellows grow louder and lower. I was used to spring fights among Charolais herd bulls in Missouri where Joe and Reggie fought on a regular basis, and once Joe had put a dent in our farm truck out of sheer frustration. Their disputes usually ended swiftly with the loser running away, a very dangerous place for anyone to be near because a bull will run over anything in his way during a retreat.

George and Ranger bellowed and butted heads and pushed and shoved and grew more weary every minute. They backed into the chain link fence and flattened part of it, which didn't curtail their fight one bit. They pushed and shoved around our house until they were within inches of the large studio window. For a second I thought they would crash inside and continue the fight in my room among the Navajo rugs and unfinished manuscripts! But luckily they turned and resumed the fight in the pasture, with no signs of stopping, as I thought they surely would. They seemed angrier than Joe and Reggie had ever been! This battle went on for over an hour. Finally George defended his territory and drove Ranger away, severely injured by a piece of projecting metal in the chain link fence that had pierced his chest. Bob loaded him up in the trailer and took him to the vet in Prescott but there was nothing that could be done for him. The metal had gone into his heart. Our beautiful Ranger gave his life as a result of the wound. Bob was heartsick.

"Why didn't you try to stop the fight?" Bob asked me. I was speechless. Stop a bull fight? Hosing them down with cold water hadn't fazed them one bit! I was glad he hadn't been home when it occurred. No doubt he would have tried to stop them. This was not the time for me to ask why he'd allowed two herd bulls to range so close together without a dividing fence. I didn't ask him, then or later.

The next spring the calves Ranger had sired began to arrive. Beauties they were, but seeing them was bittersweet. We would keep his heifers in our herd while we were on the ranch. Later we hauled several of them to a pasture we'd leased from Dale Balow on Tonto Flats, south of Prescott.

And George? We moved him to be with Ranger's daughters. We just couldn't give up our lifestyle completely. We just couldn't.

CHAPTER FORTY-TWO

Selling Out

'd always thought I'd live on the Hozoni the rest of my life. But Bob and Mike decided to sell the ranch. I was heartbroken.

Realtors came with endless buyers and I served pot after pot of cowboy coffee with a heavy heart, always wondering which person would buy the ranch and live in my beloved home. This dragged on for quite a spell, with several near sales, until we were exhausted, and then we would take it off the market for a while. We needed a rest. I was tired out from showing the house to potential buyers, and nervous exhaustion, always having it in good order by 10:00 a.m.

Bob decided Mom, he and I should spend the winter in Wickenburg, Arizona, on the desert, in a rented house owned by our long-time friends, Dr. and Aeola Mitchell. The acreage had a double-wide mobile home beautifully furnished with antiques. Out back there was a small barn and corral for Josh and Snip who we planned to trail ride on desert trails. Our house pets, Pup and Suzie, would be safe in the large dog pen.

So we loaded the animals up; horse and mule in our horse trailer, which Snip took a dislike to, and gave us trouble loading; dogs in the camper along with suitcases and a few cooking and baking pans. The plans were perfect, the results disastrous! I was homesick for the ranch and so were the dogs whose tempers were short, and frequent midnight quarrels and howls occurred until I'd shuffle out in robe and slippers to scold Pup for biting Suzie. My temper was short too, I'm sorry to say. But Bob loved it in Wickenburg and drove to the saddleshop to visit every weekday morning, then he'd come back to pick Mom and me up and drive to the adult center for lunch, which was outstanding. Mom loved it there and enjoyed visiting with people.

Josh was restless and bored. He missed the freedom of our large horse pasture and home and being confined brought out rebellious actions—he chewed on the wooden corral fence and even threatened to buck with Bob, who was in no condition for such pranks because he was recovering from an illness, that had been the purpose of our desert stay.

Trail riding plans were canceled repeatedly; Josh's naughty side grew daily. It was a mess! Once again our plans seemed to have a mind of their own.

We asked Mike not to disclose our whereabouts and he didn't, but realtors tracked us down anyway and sometimes we had to drive up the ranch to answer a potential buyer's questions and disclose my bookkeeping of cattle prices, weights, etc. Each time I prayed the ranch wouldn't sell, a newcomer wouldn't move in to my beloved old ranch house.

Finally our stay in Wickenburg ended and we loaded up and drove home. It was early spring now and I would be camping at the Robert's Line Camp soon, a comforting thought indeed.

When Bob unloaded Josh at home the poor fellow was so delighted that he dove into a dried manure pile and rolled in it! Pup and Suzie charged through the house, circling the living room and kitchen before snuggling down on their favorite rugs, located between Bob's and my chairs. Ah, home! Tears of joy rolled down my cheeks. We were home again. For how long I didn't know, but now I was home and I would enjoy every day! Maybe the men would change their minds about selling out. Maybe. . .

The next fall Tara would get on the little yellow school bus with Todd, each carrying shiny new lunch boxes Mom had bought them.

We continued to show the ranch. But then we learned that the Walnut Grove School was closing and the children would be bussed 26 miles to Kirkland which would require an early boarding on the school bus. Far too early for little ones and their day would be long by the time they arrived home. Mike moved his family closer to the Kirkland School and went to work at the TK Bar Ranch, which he later ran.

Bob, Mom and I remained on the ranch and continued showing it. Bob hired a number of cowboys for spring and fall roundups. And then came Bill, an outstanding cowboy who had a special way with horses.

Several months later we sold out. I remember we were outside Kitty Balow's café in Kirkland when we learned our realtor had called her leaving a message for us. The ranch had sold. She also said her husband Dale would sub-lease a pasture for some of our cattle, and horses, if we were interested. I felt a flood of relief. Bob had ranched too long to quit now. . .but fate had other plans.

Bill helped us with the cattle count. He was with Bob when the last cow was being loaded for Tonto Flats. Suddenly she whirled and turned back, hitting the gate where Bob was standing. It hit him and he fell backwards, knocking him unconscious. Bill gave him artificial respiration and drove him home. I remember Bill saying, "Bob's had an accident; help me get him in the house." It's chilling to recall it, even now.

Bob leaned back in his favorite chair while I hurriedly packed a few things for the hospital. There I learned his injury was very serious. He would not be able to ride horseback nor drive his truck due to poor balance, and when he attempted to he drove into the ditch.

Bob came to tell me that he and Bill were going ahead with the horses. "I'll see you at Tonto Flats," he said.

"We're going out on the green!" I said as I kissed him. He grinned at me in reply, a sad, brave smile. Going out on the green. . .his lifelong fear of droughting out had not happened. We were going out on the green. Peaceful Valley had green feed for the beautiful crossbred cattle we had sold to the ranch buyer. We'd counted them out, keeping only George and 25 gorgeous charbray cows we would pasture close to our new home, where we could see them daily. It had been almost a last-minute decision but we just couldn't sell them all.

I returned to my frantic packing. The movers were loaded and I was running late. I finished the last of my cleaning. Then I went down to ask Mom if she was ready to go. Neither of us was. My feet walked away but my heart stayed behind. At sundown Mom and I drove away from Hozoni with three frightened cowdogs howling in the horse trailer. Ahead lay Tonto Flats and my ill husband. Ahead was supper waiting for us. I knew it would be delicious. Kitty Balow's food always was.

I didn't look back into my valley as we left it there in the twilight. It would always be with me in memory. I would never have to say good-bye.

I was glad we had taken cattle and horses to Tonto Flats. They would be a comfort to Bob. . .and me.

PHOTO ALBUM

Bob in front of the Goodwin Relay Stage Station; The ox yoke was used by my family on the ox cart from Albany, New York to Michigan in 1836. It's still in the family.

Bob and Josh.

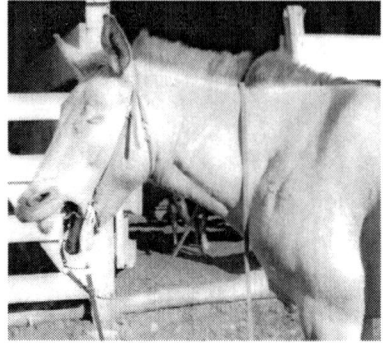

Josh getting the last laugh on the Hozoni.

Jettie and Allie Schiffer.

Bob and the gentle Gorgeous George

Dale and Kitty Balow of Tonto Flats and Skull Valley, 1986.

Bob riding Steamboat and Mike riding Smokie.

Doc and Aeola Mitchell.

Tonto Flats pasture and our cattle as viewed from our new home.

Old corral, windmill, and pasture on Tonto Flats.

Elaine, Todd and Tayleen.

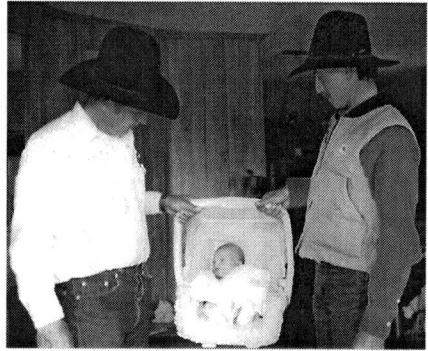

Mike, Tayleen and proud father Todd.

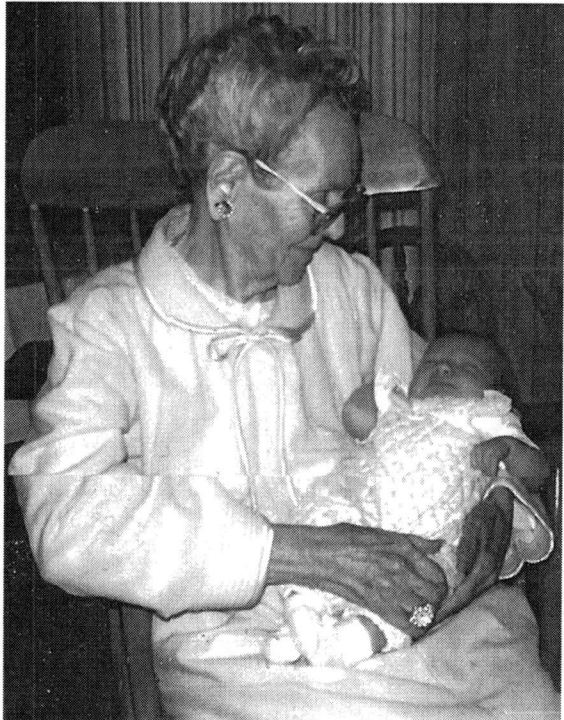

Margrey Williams and her first great-great-grandchild Tayleen White

Mom, Dad, and myself in my Easter dress -- I loved it!!
First heels, too! 1943.

About the Author

Joyce White is the author of two previous books, *Burro Creek Canyon* and *Mountain Echoes*. This third book in the series relates her life on the second Arizona cattle ranch, the Hozoni.

Joyce White passed away on March 16, 2011 at her home in Tyrone, New Mexico. She was born on September 20, 1927, and was a country person all her life, having lived on a dairy farm in Michigan, a poultry farm in southern California, a stock farm in Missouri, and two cattle ranches in Arizona. Of all the country settings she knew, it was the remote ranch life she enjoyed the most. Her move to Burro Creek Canyon in northwest Arizona in 1956 rekindled her earlier interest in writing, and in 1969 her first story was accepted by *The Western Horseman*.

Her researched articles and reflections have appeared in American Horseman, Outdoor Arizona, and Bottles and Relics. She wrote a weekly column, "Ranch Echoes", for the Silver City Sun-News.

She was a descendant of two pioneer families: the Fairbanks who gave us the Fairbanks Scales and lent their name to Fairbanks, Alaska and Fairbanks, Arizona, and produced the actor Douglas Fairbanks, Jr. and a vice-president of the United States, Charles Warren Fairbanks. She was a direct descendent of Brigham Young, the second president of the Church of Jesus Christ of Latter-day Saints.

Joyce White's grave at the rim of Burro Creek Canyon.

Eulogy

Joyce White's grave, pictured above, is at the rim of Burro Creek Canyon. Shown to the right are her son Michael Earl White and her great-grandson Huston Koester.
Her grandson Michael Todd White welded the cross together out of old horseshoes and his father Mike carved her name into the flagstone plaque.

To the far left you can see fifteen-hundred feet below to the ranch house built by Bob White, where Mike grew up as a boy and Joyce fell in love forever with Burro Creek Canyon.

Visitors who brave the long, rough trip to her grave are asked to bring a rock from wherever in the world they come from to pile alongside her grave as a memorial monument.

Joyce White was beloved by a vast multitude of people throughout the world for her gentle nature and unquestioned character that serves as an elevated example for the human species.

Her authentic, historical and inspiring writing about western rough county cattle ranching depicts all the virtues that made our country great. Her writing is something to be eternally proud of as it gives us hope for the future, and that we can be a better human being than each of us thought possible.

I was but one of the many who loved Joyce White and was truly humbled by the realization that she could in return love me in spite of all my inadequacies, faults and shortcomings. That so grand, compassionate and talented a person could see any value or quality in me justifies my very existence in this world as nothing else ever did or could.

At the sight of one of her books, an old column, a scribbled note among her working manuscripts or any trivial object that brings her to mind again, I still choke and mist up even now as I write this, for Joyce White truly was an authentic gentle lady of the old west, the likes of which we will not soon see again, and for that, I grieve.

Derrall D. Horn, Publisher

35 Ranch-Tested Recipes

CPSIA information can be obtained at www.ICGtesting.com
Printed in the USA
LVOW132349090113

315123LV00002B/8/P

9 780979 366727